A Chosen Faith

Dear Miranda,

Welcome to First Parish in Sherborn! Looking forward to sharing the journey.

— Nathan —

A CHOSEN FAITH

♦

*An Introduction to
Unitarian Universalism*

Revised Edition

♦

*John A. Buehrens and
Forrest Church*

♦

*New Foreword by Robert Fulghum
New Preface by Denise Davidoff*

BEACON PRESS ♦ BOSTON

Beacon Press
25 Beacon Street
Boston, Massachusetts 02108-2892
www.beacon.org

Beacon Press books
are published under the auspices of
the Unitarian Universalist Association of
Congregations.

11 10   16 15
This book is printed on acid-free paper that meets the
uncoated paper ANSI/NISO specifications for perma-
nence as revised in 1992.
Text design by Lisa Diercks

Library of Congress Cataloging-in-Publication Data
Buehrens, John A.
A chosen faith : an introduction to Unitarian
Universalism /
John A. Buehrens and Forrest Church ; new foreward
by Robert Fulghum ; new preface by Denise Davidoff.
- Rev. ed.
p.   cm.
Rev. ed. of: Our chosen faith. © 1989
Includes bibliographical references (p.).
ISBN 978-08070-1617-6

I. Unitarian Universalist churches-Doctrines. I.
Church, F. Forrester.
II. Buehrens, John A., 1947-   Our chosen faith.
III. Title.
BX9841.2.B84   1998
230'.9132-dc21   97-51479

*To Gwen Langdoc Buehrens, Amy Furth,
and George Hunston Williams*

Contents

CONTENTS

Foreword

HERE'S PART OF a conversation in a bookstore:

"Mr. Fulghum, is it true that you're a minister?"

"Yes."

"Where's your church?"

"We're standing in it."

"But this is a bookstore and it's a Friday."

"Yes, but you might also choose to see it as a cathedral of the human spirit—a storehouse consecrated to the full spectrum of human experience. Just about every idea we've ever had is in here somewhere. A place containing great thinking is a sacred space."

"Really? Just what kind of minister are you?"

"Unitarian Universalist."

"And you hold services in bookstores on Fridays? You're putting me on."

"No, but I am giving you an example of how Unitarian Universalists think. More than anything else, our religion is defined by an attitude. An open-minded point of view. About everything and anything. What we have most in common is an uncommon way of looking at the obvious. A church is not just a specific building, but also a way of looking at the building you're in at the moment. A minister is not just a person who stands in a pulpit and preaches on Sunday mornings, but also the way some people engage the world. A religion is not contained in a single book; there's something religious in almost any book."

"OK, but I've seen a building in my neighborhood with a sign that says 'Unitarian Universalist Church' on it and there are a lot of cars parked around it on Sunday mornings. Looks like a regular church to me."

"Of course. We come together in community and do many things any religious community does—and Sunday mornings are a culturally convenient time to meet. But we also come together during the rest of the week."

"To do what?"

"To share ideas, discuss political action, work on projects of benefit to the larger community in which we live, and hear speakers on a broad range of topics. We enjoy and need the companionship of like-minded people."

"Mr. Fulghum, I've read all your books. Is what you write a sample of what Unitarian Universalists believe?"

"Yes and no. I would expect, and hope, that most Unitarian Universalists would not agree with everything I think and write."

"You mean there's no party line—no dogma?"

"Yes and no. We agree that individuals must work out their own religious conclusions. We agree that we will disagree on those conclusions. We agree to respect those differences. We agree to learn from one another through dialogue about our beliefs. We agree on a process and the tools to be used in the process."

"Give me some examples of the tools."

"The principles of democracy, integrity, continuing education, and individual responsibility, to name a few."

"It sounds more like NPR or PBS to me than a church."

"Actually, the analogy is not far off. Public radio and public television are good examples of things that Unitarian Universalists support. We want to be exposed to a wide range of information and a broad range of viewpoints. We want each individual to have an influence on programming, and we want each individual to take responsibility for keeping the programs on the air. It's not the easiest way to go about radio or religious community, but it's the way we choose."

"So if I'm open-minded and listen to NPR and watch PBS, I qualify as a Unitarian Universalist?"

"Let's say you have Unitarian Universalist tendencies. There are, however, Unitarian Universalists who listen only to jazz or country-western music or opera, or those who watch only baseball on TV. I say again, we respect diversity in all things."

"What about politics?"

"No exception. Full spectrum. Democrats, Republicans, Libertarians, Socialists, and a few who are either Anarchists or just confused—it's hard to tell. We share only the conviction that one ought to be active in the affairs of the world. We don't dictate which particular party one ought to join."

"Are Unitarian Universalists Christians?"

"Again, yes and no. Some are and some aren't, and some haven't decided. Same answer if you ask whether Unitarian Universalists are Buddhists. In fact, most of the specific questions you might ask have this kind of answer. Yes and no. Some are and some aren't. Some do and some don't. We're known for respecting diversity of opinion and belief."

"I'd like to come take a look at a church like that, but I don't want to get put on your missionary list."

"No problem. We don't evangelize. We keep a door open to those who are looking for the company of people like us. We find there are a great many people who are Unitarian Universalists and don't know it. When we ask most Unitarian Universalists how they came to be members, they say it's because they were looking for a community of people who are liberal in their religious values and active in their commitment to community service. We believe in the right of the individual to choose religious principles and in the individual's responsibility to put those principles into practice."

"I'd like to know more."

What you've just read is a reconstruction of an awkward conversation I've had many times. It's hard to summarize one's beliefs in a few moments—they're products of a lifetime's experience. Hard, also, to give a short historical perspective of Unitarian Universalism because it too is long and rich and deep. If you want to have better answers to your questions about our chosen faith, read further in this book. If you really want to know what it means to be a Unitarian Universalist, come see what we are and what we do—you may be one of us.

Robert Fulghum

Preface

MY HUSBAND, JERRY, and I discovered the Unitarian Universalist church in Westport, Connecticut, in the winter of 1960. We liked the people. We liked the Sunday morning worship in the Saugatuck School auditorium. We liked the potluck suppers. We *loved* the minister, Arnold Westwood. Even three-year-old Douglass liked the place. It seemed like a perfect fit.

Sounds easy, you say. But it wasn't. Signing the membership book in a Unitarian church was scary beyond belief for me even to contemplate. How would I tell my parents I was rejecting the faith of my forefathers? (Yes, fore*fathers*! Remember, this was 1960.) I don't just mean my Jewish grandfathers Louis Taft and Harry Zuckerman, who had emigrated from the Ukraine in the late nineteenth century. I mean those *other* forefathers: Abraham, Isaac, and Jacob. How would I tell my aunts and uncles and cousins? How would I tell my in-laws? How would I tell our friends, particularly those in the Temple Israel community in our town?

And *what* would I tell them? Who had a vocabulary in the early sixties to express the stifling bonds of patriarchy I felt in the synagogue? How could I express feelings of exclusion and put-down I later came to know as feminist? How to explain how good that simple English language liturgy and those guilt-free, uplifting sermons felt in the ears and, increasingly, in the heart? Emerson and Channing and Parker were names mentioned in courses I'd taken in American cultural history at Vassar. But join a *church*? (In my family, if you went to a church, you were a Christian. Many still don't believe me when I tell them that, while some Unitarian Universalists are Christians, many others claim other commitments and traditions.) Leave the family? Deal with Dad's wrath, Mom's tears, and my brother's bewilderment? Was I crazy?

Yes, it was scary. And it took me six and a half years to sign that book. By that time, I was teaching in the Sunday School, serving on committees, canvassing for the pledge drive, and reveling in the beautiful contemporary building we had built on Lyons Plains Road. But even then, all those years later, I still couldn't articulate this newfound faith of mine. The journey to articulation would take much longer than I could ever have imagined. To be truthful, it continues to this day.

Most of us who are active Unitarian Universalists

don't know anything close to "enough" about our faith. We often don't understand where the Unitarian Universalist Association came from and, as a result, we cannot have a vision of where we might go. We struggle to speak our Unitarian Universalism to each other and, particularly, to the interfaith world beyond the walls of our societies. We get frustrated trying to explain the theological underpinnings of our social witness to ourselves or to the people with whom we share that witness. We are hampered by our ignorance. We are fettered by our lack of theological education. How could people who value learning so much find themselves knowing so little? *A Chosen Faith* has helped change that.

I delight to see that Unitarian Universalists are moving into the interfaith world, forging and joining coalitions to fight for the rights of others, to engage the radical religious right in the political arena, to stand for and seek ways to institutionalize antiracism. We do this work because our religious faith demands it of us. We do this work with others because we recognize that we are too small to do it effectively by ourselves. We do this work because we want people to know that Unitarian Universalists prefer to fight against the world's oppressions with other people of faith.

If you are a Unitarian Universalist, this book can help speak your faith. I promise that you will find it an exhilarating experience. When you stumble, go back and read it again. It is so very important that a weary and cynical world know more about our healing message and our unabashed liberal religious spirit. We can all be the message carriers. And this, my sisters and brothers, will be good.

If you are not (or not *yet*) a Unitarian Universalist, you will learn more about who we are, and *why* we are, from these pages. And you may even learn more about yourself and your own religious journey.

Enjoy, enjoy!

Denise Taft Davidoff
Moderator, Unitarian Universalist Association

Introduction

Forrest Church

ALL THEOLOGY IS autobiography. As are most sweeping generalizations, this one is false. Yet it does provide a useful hook for ministers who enjoy talking about themselves.

The most recent minister to stake this claim is a Presbyterian, but he is also a novelist, which may explain his fascination with "the flesh made word." His name is Frederick Buechner. I enjoy his novels and number him among my favorite theologians—not that I always agree with him. After all, I was a Presbyterian myself once.

When I attended Sunday school—irregularly, I must confess—the difference between good and bad Presbyterians was clear. Good Presbyterians chose the right colors and stayed inside the lines. But I was a bad Presbyterian for more important reasons than my lack of artistic talent; I did not believe what I was being taught. So I left the Presbyterian church, wandered for a time, and then, happily, became a Unitarian Universalist. This was an act of kindness to the Presbyterians as much as to myself. After all, the Presbyterian church is full of bad Presbyterians. The last thing in the world they need is another one.

Equating theology and autobiography may be somewhat facile, but less so perhaps for Unitarian Universalists than for followers of other faiths. For most of us, our faith did not choose us, we chose it. Born Catholic, Jewish, Protestant, Muslim, or into a secular or "mixed" household, when it came time for us to affiliate with a religious institution we sought one that fit our own thinking, not one that imposed its thinking on us. This is even true for individuals born into Unitarian Universalist families. In our religious education programs, though we place special emphasis on liberal religious traditions and values, we also introduce our children to many different religious and theological approaches, encouraging them to formulate their own beliefs and make their own commitments.

Unitarian Universalists are neither a chosen people nor a people whose choices are made for them by theological authorities—ancient or otherwise. We are a people who choose. Ours is a faith whose authority is grounded in contemporary experience, not ancient revelation. Thought we find ourselves naturally drawn to the teachings of our adopted religious forebears, these teachings echo with new insights, insights of our own. Ralph Waldo Emerson did not seek disciples; he sought people who could use their minds and tap their souls as profoundly as he did. In a Unitarian Universalist church, revelation is an ongoing process; each of us is a potential harbinger of meaning.

In this spirit, what follows is very much a personal introduction to Unitarian Universalism. The light of our shared faith is refracted through two prisms. John Buehrens and I lay no claim to objectivity, yet by writing this work together we hope that the results are at least a bit less subjective than if either of us had attempted the task alone.

At All Souls Unitarian Church in New York City, the church we were privileged to serve together as ministers, John was the rabbi to my evangelist. This is not the only way our styles differ. Emerson once divided authors into two categories, spiders and bees. By such a measure, I am a spider who spins what he has to say out of himself; John is more of a bee flitting from flower to flower gathering nectar. As my wife once indelicately put it, "You and John complement each other perfectly. You write. He reads."

We have written this book together for another reason. If you ask what Unitarian Universalists believe, two answers, especially if they vary, are almost certainly better than one. In our circle of faith, when two or more gather, a loving argument is a sure sign that the spirit is moving among us.

Yet far more unites than divides us. Unitarian Universalist minister David Rankin, minister of the Fountain Street Church in Grand Rapids, Michigan, lists ten beliefs we hold in common.

1. We believe in the freedom of religious expression. All individuals should be encouraged to develop a personal theology, and to openly present their religious opinions without fear of censure or reprisal.

2. We believe in tolerance of religious ideas. The religions of every age and culture have something to teach those who listen.

3. We believe in the authority of reason and conscience. The ultimate arbiter in religion is not a church, a document, or an official, but the personal choice and decision of the individual.

4. We believe in the search for truth. With an open mind and heart, there is no end to the fruitful and exciting revelations that the human spirit can find.

5. We believe in the unity of experience. There is no fundamental conflict between faith and knowledge; religion and the world; the sacred and the secular.

6. We believe in the worth and dignity of each human being. All people on earth have an equal

claim to life, liberty, and justice; no idea, ideal, or philosophy is superior to a single human life.

7. We believe in the ethical application of religion. Inner grace and faith finds completion in social and community involvement.

8. We believe in the force of love, that the governing principle in human relationships is the principle of love, which seeks to help and heal, never to hurt or destroy.

9. We believe in the necessity of the democratic process. Records are open to scrutiny, elections are open to members, and ideas are open to criticism, so that people might govern themselves.

10. We believe in the importance of a religious community. Peers confirm and validate experience, and provide a critical platform, as well as a network of mutual support.

We have no explicit creed, either theological or social, to guide us. Yet when one considers these basic points of agreement, it is no surprise that Unitarians and Universalists (the two denominations merged in 1961 to form the Unitarian Universalist Association) have often led the march for equality and social justice. In the following pages we will meet Unitarian Universalist laypersons and ministers who have been instrumental in promoting American independence, public education and health care, social services to the poor, abolition of slavery, animal rights, suffrage for women, civil rights for minorities, the rights and dignity of homosexuals, and women's equality.

Rankin's list is one individual's view of the beliefs we hold in common, not a consensus statement. We do have such a statement, however. And it was inspired not by the men, but by the women in our movement. This is not unusual given our long tradition of supporting an equal voice for women in all human endeavor. Not only does our denomination have a larger percentage of women ministers than any other (today some 60 percent of our candidates for ministry are women), but ours was also the first to officially sanction a woman minister (Olympia Brown in 1863). In the same great tradition, it was a group of women, lay and ordained, who headed the campaign for a revision of our denominational bylaws. Over three years and through a democratic process we incorporated the thoughts of Unitarian Universalists in churches and fellowships throughout the United States and Canada. The following statement of principles, enacted by the General Assembly of 1986, captures the essence of our common faith.

We, the member congregations of the Unitarian Universalist Association, covenant to affirm and promote:
• The inherent worth and dignity of every person;
• Justice, equity, and compassion in human relations;

- Acceptance of one another and encouragement to spiritual growth in our congregations;
- A free and responsible search for truth and meaning;
- The rights of conscience and the use of the democratic process within our congregations and in society at large;
- The goal of world community with peace, liberty, and justice for all;
- Respect for the interdependent web of all existence, of which we are a part.

In addition to our principles, the covenant of our association as now codified in our bylaws also refers to the six sources of our faith, with reference to which this introduction to Unitarian Universalism is structured:

The living tradition we share draws from many sources:
- Direct experience of that transcending mystery and wonder, affirmed in all cultures, which moves us to a renewal of the spirit and an openness to the forces that create and uphold life;
- Words and deeds of prophetic women and men, which challenge us to confront powers and structures of evil with justice, compassion, and the transforming power of love;
- Wisdom from the world's religions, which inspires us in our ethical and spiritual life;

- Jewish and Christian teachings, which call us to respond to God's love by loving our neighbors as ourselves;
- Humanist teachings, which counsel us to heed the guidance of reason and the results of science, and warn us against idolatries of the mind and spirit;
- Spiritual teachings of Earth-centered traditions, which celebrate the sacred circle of life and instruct us to live in harmony with the rhythms of nature.

John, now president of the UUA, and I will explore each of these sources in turn, weaving personal stories, tales from denominational and liberal religious history, and wisdom gained from those we have been blessed to serve over the past decade and a half in Unitarian Universalist congregations across the United States: in Summit, New Jersey; Knoxville, Tennessee; Dallas, Texas; Boston and Lexington, Massachusetts; and New York City.

In some respects this book is unusual for its genre. To introduce our history and theology we employ a form of free association, alighting here and there according to theme, rather than presenting facts in a linear progression. Furthermore, because we draw heavily from personal experience, the churches we have served receive disproportionate attention, as do our individual prejudices. By the same token, unlike most such works, this one is not uncritical. We celebrate our faith, of course, but also attempt independently to judge our faithfulness to it.

Our special thanks to Wendy Strothman, former director of Beacon Press, for her willingness to commission a new introduction to Unitarian Universalism, yet another expression of her commitment to expanding the ideas and ideals of liberal religion, and to Beacon's new director, Helene Atwan, who welcomed this revised edition. Both were extremely generous in their encouragement and helpful in their criticism as this project unfolded. In addition to our editor, Susan Worst, we are also indebted to several people who read an early typescript and made suggestions for improving it: James Luther Adams; Khoren Arisian; Mark Belletini; Denise Davidoff; Gordon McKeeman; Susan Milnor; Mark Morrison-Reed; Judith Walker-Riggs; Edward Simmons; Terry Sweetser; and John Wolf. We did not accept all their emendations, so none shares the blame for what may be wrong here, but all are partially responsible for what is right. Parts of the first chapter are adapted from my 1980 lectures, *Born Again Unitarian Universalism*, which happily this introduction to our faith will now supplant.

This revised edition contains two new chapters, each focusing on earth-centered religious traditions. Our faith continues to grow and change with changing times. That is why we both chose it.

*The living tradition we share draws
from many sources. . .*

PART I

Direct experience of that transcending mystery and wonder, affirmed in all cultures, which moves us to a renewal of the spirit and an openness to the forces that create and uphold life.

Awakening

Forrest Church

Small as is our whole system compared with the infinitude of creation, brief as is our life compared with the cycles of time, we are so tethered to all by the beautiful dependencies of law, that not only the sparrow's fall is felt to the outermost bound, but the vibrations set in motion by the words that we utter reach through all space and the tremor is felt through all time.

—Maria Mitchell, nineteenth-century Unitarian and astronomer

I can believe a miracle because I can raise my own arm. I can believe a miracle because I can remember. I can believe it because I can speak and be understood by you.

—Ralph Waldo Emerson, Unitarian minister and essayist

MY FIRST SIGNIFICANT religious experience took place when I was about ten years old. As I look back on it, I recognize that in form this experience was typically

Unitarian Universalist. I was reading a book. Perhaps more surprisingly, that book was the Bible.

I had already read bits and pieces of the Bible before. Having attended Presbyterian Sunday school, I was acquainted in broad outline with its principal characters and plot. Admittedly, the coloring book approach to the Bible was the one I knew best. Lots of sheep, as I remember, and men wearing bathrobes. The little I might have gained from this narrow approach was further limited by my appalling lack of artistic talent. I knew enough not to color Jesus blue, but had a terrible time keeping the sky out of his face. In any event, my early endeavors in religion merited me a small red, not a large gold, star. It was not until my father presented me with my own Bible, all words and no pictures, that things began to change.

The Bible my father gave me was a very peculiar one. It was the Jefferson Bible, *The Life and Morals of Jesus of Nazareth.* As I later learned, near the end of his first term in the White House, Thomas Jefferson abstracted from the four Gospels his own version of Jesus' life and teachings. Carefully excising all miracles, most of the narrative, and any of Jesus' words that offended his "enlightened" sensibilities, Jefferson pieced together a little volume containing what he believed were the essential teachings of Jesus. It opens with Mary already great with child—no mention is made of any extraordinary circumstances surrounding the conception. It closes with an account of Jesus' crucifixion, death, and burial. The final words in Jefferson's Bible are these: "There laid they Jesus, and rolled a great stone to the door of the sepulchre, and departed."

What an extraordinary revelation for a ten-year-old boy, a boy who knew how the story was *supposed* to turn out. The resurrection was missing. This story, the tale of God's son preaching salvation and proclaiming the advent of the Realm of God, ended in the ordinary all-too-human way: Having for a brief time lived, even having loved and served so well and memorably, the hero died.

This realization is the first of many awakenings that have shaped my understanding of what religion means: *Religion is our human response to the dual reality of being alive and having to die.* Knowing we are going to die not only places an acknowledged limit upon our lives, it also gives a special intensity and poignancy to the time we are given to live and love. The fact that death is inevitable gives meaning to our love, for the more we love the more we risk losing. Love's power comes in part from the courage required to give ourselves to that which is not ours to keep: our spouses, children, parents, dear and cherished friends, even life itself. It also comes from the faith required to sustain that courage, the faith that life, howsoever limited and mysterious, contains within its margins, often at their very edges, a meaning that is redemptive.

With Jesus, resurrection or no resurrection, that was demonstrably the case: He lived in such a way that his life proved to be worth dying for. And yet, from the Apostles' Creed, embraced as doctrine throughout much of Christendom, one would have little way of knowing this. Here is what the Apostles' Creed has to say concerning Jesus:

I believe in God, the Father Almighty, Creator of heaven and earth, and in Jesus Christ, His only Son, our Lord, who was conceived by the Holy Spirit, born of the Virgin Mary, suffered under Pontius Pilate, was crucified, died, and was buried, descended to hell, on the third day rose again from the dead, ascended to heaven, sits at the right hand of God, the Father Almighty, whence He will come to judge the living and the dead.

What does this creed affirm about Jesus' life and teachings? Not one thing. It states merely that he was born in an unusual way and died in an unusual way, telling us nothing about the fact that Jesus *lived* in an unusual way. This is what is important about Jesus. Not that he existed before he was born; was implanted in a virgin's womb; visited hell after he died; and then returned to be resurrected and reign in heaven. These are dogmatic propositions of faith. They can be confirmed by faith alone, and a mighty leap of faith at that, for they stand in direct contradiction to nature's laws.

One question often asked of Unitarian Universalists is, Are you Christian? Our faith does have Christian roots, many of us gather in churches (others prefer the terms congregation, society, or fellowship), and some of our members call themselves Christians. But whatever we call ourselves (Christian, Jew, theist, agnostic, humanist, atheist), most of us would agree that the important thing about Jesus is not his supposed miraculous birth or the claim that he was resurrected from death, but rather how he *lived*. The power of his love, the penetrating simplicity of his teachings, and the force of his example of service on behalf of the disenfranchised and downtrodden are what is crucial. The Apostles' Creed and other such statements of dogmatic theology entirely miss this point. They seem to suggest "if you believe in Jesus, you can live forever," not, "if you believe as Jesus, you can live well."

Of course, I am a heretic. The word *hairesis* in Greek means choice; a heretic is one who is able to choose. Its root stems from the Greek verb *hairein,* to take. Faced with the mystery of life and death, each act of faith is a gamble. We all risk choices before the unknown.

Pascal popularized the notion of the wager with respect to religion. He argued that one could gamble on there being an afterlife or not. Admittedly, raised in a Christian culture, he remained convinced that the odds were with him. But even if they were not, it was a good bet. After all, if he was wrong, he lost nothing. After he died, if his life was extinguished it would make no difference whether he had believed in an afterlife or not. But if he was right, it was golden, everlasting bliss. Who would be fool enough not to risk a wager where you could lose nothing if you were wrong, but could gain eternal life if you were right?

I am one such fool. I simply cannot accept Pascal's wager. Faith may be a gamble in face of the unknown, but religion is not a game. We do not play it, we live it. I have no idea what will happen to me when I die, but I know that I will die. And I know that the choices I make in this life affect the way I live. It is in this crucible, mysterious and uncertain, that my religion must be forged.

As Unitarian Universalists, we are free to choose our beliefs. This is evident from our first source: "Direct experience of that transcending mystery and wonder, affirmed in all cultures, which moves us to a renewal of the spirit and an openness to the forces that create and uphold life." Of course, being free, we are responsible for what we make of that freedom. Freedom may be our forge, but responsibility remains the anvil on which our faith is pounded out and turned to use. With this one caution, the main difference between a faith drawn from direct experience and one founded on revelation lies only in the source of our beliefs, not in their respective transformational or redemptive power. When we employ our freedom responsibly, directly experiencing the transcending mystery and wonder of the creation, our spirits are renewed and we become open to the forces that create and uphold life.

The difference between a Unitarian Universalist approach to religion and that of traditional Christianity (our culture's most familiar benchmark) is graphically demonstrated in an exchange of letters between D. H. Lawrence, the famous British novelist, and his mother's pastor. When Lawrence was a young man, he exchanged letters with the Reverend Robert Reid. Reid served the Congregational church of Eastwood, where Lawrence worshiped as a boy. When Lawrence left home for school, Mrs. Lawrence, worrying about the state of her son's soul, prevailed upon her pastor to send Lawrence a selection of his sermons. The author's response to one of these survives. Apparently, it was a sermon on the necessity of conversion for salvation. Lawrence answered:

I believe that one is converted when first one hears the low, vast murmur of life, of human life, troubling one's hitherto unconscious self. I believe one is born first unto oneself—for the happy developing of oneself, while the world is a nursery, and the pretty things are to be snatched for, and the pleasant things tasted; some people seem to exist thus right to the end. But most are born again on entering maturity; then they are born to humanity, to a consciousness of all the laughing, and the never-ceasing murmur of pain and sorrow that comes from the terrible multitude of brothers [and sisters]. Then, it appears to me, one gradually formulates one's religion, be it what it may. A person has no religion who has not slowly and painfully gathered one together, adding to it, shaping it; and one's religion is never complete and final, it seems, but must always be undergoing modification.

Lawrence was not a Unitarian. Nevertheless, here, in the lost yet easily reconstructed sermon of Mr. Reid and in D. H. Lawrence's response, the distinction between a Unitarian Universalist approach to religion and that of a more orthodox believer is made clear. Reid represents the traditional view. By his reading, religion is a body of specific teachings and practices, won by a leap of faith and secured by strict adherence to the truth as it is revealed or taught. In most Christian churches this means accepting Jesus Christ as Lord and Savior, the Bible as the unique revelation of God's word, and the sacraments as the unique communication of God's presence. Beyond this, there are specific requirements inherent to each of the various denominations. One group may affirm the central importance of adult baptism, or Saturday worship, another the primacy of presbyters, or bishops, or the pope. These basic requirements are so common that people outside as well as within such churches tend to accept the traditional definition of religion: a subscription to some fixed combination of doctrine and practice.

In his response to Reid's sermon, D. H. Lawrence opens a clearer, wider, and more expansive window on the subject. For him, religion has little to do with a body of beliefs or practices; it represents a gradual process of awakening to the depths and possibilities of life itself.

When Lawrence and Reid use the word conversion, they mean very different things. Reid thinks of it as "casting off the old self and putting on the new." But for Lawrence, conversion means awakening: opening our eyes, looking out with new wonder upon the creation, becoming not someone other than ourselves, but more fully ourselves. Through direct experience of transcending mystery and wonder, he was moved to "a renewal of the spirit and an openness to the forces that create and uphold life."

If religion is our human response to the dual reality of being alive and having to die, Unitarian Universalism might best be described as a life-affirming rather than death-defying faith. Yet to affirm life, we must also face death, and struggle to make sense of both.

When we are born, we perceive everything around us as an extension of ourselves. From our first breath and well before, the life force that animates and sustains us is a given. We take life for granted. Others are responsible for our being alive and remaining so—our being nourished, clothed, and sheltered. Only over time, as we grow through the pains of separation and ego development and find ourselves having to compete for affection, do we begin to awaken to the complexities of the human condition. These struggles are not easy; life is difficult. Our first temptation is to rebel against this fact, begrudging all of life's limitations, especially death as its inevitability steals into our consciousness.

Offering religious security blankets and heavenly insurance policies, many faiths base their considerable appeal on a denial of death. They reduce this life to preparation for the next, potentially finer life. I cannot accept their gambit. The price for defeating the presumed enemy is too great. By refusing to accept the dispensation of death as a condition for the gift of birth, life's intrinsic wonder and promise are diminished.

Death is a fairly recent entry in the scheme of evolution. The beginnings of life on this planet were sponsored by single cell organisms, which replicated themselves by division. One generation of beings followed another, each identical to the last. We were immortal, until we became interesting. Without death, life, in its familiar, individuated, and endlessly fascinating permutations and commutations—would simply not exist.

On the other hand, our lives are also diminished when we ignore death. For this reason, even as Unitarian Universalists, we need to be "born again." For D. H. Lawrence, to be born again has a very different connotation from that of fundamentalist Christians. It happens when we awaken to the fact that life is not a given—not something to be taken for granted, or transcended after death—but a gift, undeserved and unexpected, holy, awesome, and mysterious.

To illustrate this, I have only to repeat Ralph Waldo Emerson's words of interpretation and praise. Jesus "spoke of miracles," Emerson wrote, "for he felt that [our] life was a miracle, and all that [we do], and he knew that this daily miracle shines as [we divine it]. But the very word Miracle, as pronounced by Christian churches, gives a false impression; it is Monster. It is not one with the blowing clover and the falling rain." In Emerson's view, there is only one miracle—life itself. Elsewhere he writes:

It will not need, when the mind is prepared for study, to search for objects. The invariable mark of wisdom is to see the miraculous in the common. What is a day? What is a year? What is summer? What is woman? What is a child? What is sleep? To our blindness, these things seem unaffecting. We make fables to hide the baldness of the fact and conform it, as we say, to the higher law of the mind. [But to the wise] a fact is true poetry, and the most beautiful of fables.

If Emerson is right, and I believe he is, then to all who would divine its presence, the miracle of life, natural and unalloyed, is made manifest in every living thing. Yes, in Jesus, who indeed was a son of God—even as we each have the potential to be sons and daughters of God—and in his words and deeds, but not uniquely there. As the author of the New Testament book of Hebrews reminds us, "Some have entertained angels unawares." If angels may be defined as the incarnation of the divine in the ordinary, awakening to the miracle of life entails not so much a discovery of the supernatural, but rather a discovery of the super in the natural.

Each of us, of course, must assume the responsibility for awakening. Others may be responsible for our being born, but what we make of our lives, how deeply and intensively we live, is our responsibility, and ours alone. Having accepted life as a gift for ourselves, we are then charged to revere the presence of this same gift in others. As long as we take life for granted, our regard for it is cheapened and this affects the way we treat others, even those closest to us. Part of being born again, in a Unitarian Universalist way, lies in waking up to the fact that all of life is a gift. The world does not owe us a living, we owe the world a living, our own.

With this in mind, redemption too takes on a different connotation. Think for a moment about the marketplace meaning of redemption. We have a coupon. It is worth almost nothing in and of itself. One tenth of a cent, they say. But when we redeem that coupon, we receive something that does have intrinsic value.

The same is true of us. In and of themselves our individual lives may be worth very little, but when redeemed, they are translated into something of immeasurable value. By this interpretation, redemption has little to do with escaping death. Instead, it involves discovering and acting upon life's hidden yet abundant richness. And should we happen to graduate to another life (a possibility little more remote than that there should be life in the first place) to live well and deeply in this life must surely be the best preparation imaginable for advancing to the next.

As with all theological issues, Unitarian Universalists represent a broad spectrum of views when it comes to life after death (transmigration, resurrection, extinction, immortality). Most of us, however, view death not as something unnatural, but as a natural passage—like birth, one of the hinges upon which life turns.

Perhaps a more organic metaphor would serve even better. Barbara Holleroth, a Unitarian Universalist pastoral counselor, writes, "It is sometimes said that we are born as strangers into the world and that we leave it when we die. But in all probability we do not come into the world at all. Rather, we come out of it, in the same way that a leaf comes out of the tree or a baby from its mother's body. We emerge from deep within its range of possibilities, and when we die we do not so much stop living as take on a different form. So the leaf does not fall out of the world when it leaves the tree. It has a different way and place to be within it."

Such insights are awakenings. Awakening is not a moment, but an ongoing process. By remaining open to experiencing the mystery of life anew, we are born again and again. Each time we encounter life's transcending mystery and are moved to a renewal of the spirit and an openness to the forces that create and uphold us, we awaken.

I began awakening some forty years ago when I opened Thomas Jefferson's Bible and realized that Jesus' life was not special because he was more than human or other than human. It was special because Jesus fully realized the promise of his humanity. I had no idea then, that Thomas Jefferson had Unitarian leanings. Nor did I have the faintest inkling that I would later become a Unitarian Universalist minister. But I can see now that the seed of this life-affirming faith of ours was planted then in the heart of a ten-year-old boy.

I may no longer accept the answers offered to me by my Presbyterian Sunday school teacher. But her questions turned out to be right. Where do we come from? Who are we? Where are we going? How do we attain salvation, that is, spiritual health or wholeness? How can we live a life befitting our promise? How should we face death? And how, when our lives reach their close, can we be sure they will have been worth dying for?

2

Experience

John A. Buehrens

In every life there are certain moments which partake of another, higher order of experience—peculiarly precious moments which offer serenity, hope, and strength and which allow us to return to the demands of daily life with renewed vitality and confidence. The growth of a spiritual dimension in each of us as individuals seems to result in a multiplication and a deepening of such moments both in ourselves and in the world.

—Elizabeth M. Jones, Unitarian Universalist layperson

Sometimes our light goes out but is blown into flame by an encounter with another human being. Each of us owes the deepest thanks to those who have rekindled this inner light.
—Dr. Albert Schweitzer, member, Church of the Larger Fellowship (Unitarian Universalist)

I STILL RECALL the first time I entered a Unitarian Universalist meetinghouse. It was in the spring of 1968 and the occasion was a memorial service for Dr. Martin Luther King, Jr. The place was Cambridge, Massachusetts, where I was then a senior at Harvard. Much of what was said I no longer remember. But I do recall staring at the plaque that hung next to the chancel. It said, "What doth the Lord require of thee but to do justice, to love mercy, and to walk humbly with thy God?" (Mic. 6:8).

A prophet had been killed again. But as someone said that day, the prophets can only really die, or lose their influence, if we stop asking the tough questions they pose—questions God might be asking of us. Instead, we avoid such uncomfortable ideas by focusing on what *we* might require—in a faith, a cause, a tradition, a God.

At the age of twenty-one, like many people, I had grown away from conventional religion. My mother had raised me a nominal Roman Catholic. My father, a former Protestant, had little use for religion at all. The failures of religion were clear to me. It fails existentially when it suppresses our individual questions and doubts and when it implies that our experience must fit some predetermined pattern. It fails socially when it becomes superficial, pleasingly aesthetic, or fashionably political. Yet I also knew that mere secular existence often does little better. I had a yearning for community and transcendent values. In short, I wanted an honest religion, one that could both, as Reinhold

Niebuhr once said, "afflict the comfortable and comfort the afflicted." But I could hardly have expressed that yearning then.

I had a black roommate, whom I admired, who had been raised in a Unitarian Universalist family and congregation. He had been president of the continental organization of Liberal Religious Youth and was president of our class at Harvard. (He had invited Dr. King to be our Class Day speaker at graduation—Coretta King came instead). Through him, I learned about the contributions of Unitarian Universalists to social reform.

Through George Huntston Williams, a Unitarian Universalist historian for whom I did research that year, I was also learning about the intellectual and spiritual roots of the tradition—in Europe, among Renaissance humanists and the more radical wing of the Reformation; in America, among descendents of the early Pilgrims and Puritans, promoters of American independence, and leaders of the New England cultural renaissance of the 1800s. Of course, I would not have said a tradition attracted me. I thought it was the individuals. Like many of my age and generation, that was what I wanted to be—an individual. And that, I thought, meant a break with all tradition—going my own way, in life and in faith.

Yet sitting in that historic meetinghouse, I could hear the words of Emerson, who I knew had spoken there. "Why should not we enjoy an original relation to the universe?" he had asked. "Why should not we have poetry and philosophy of insight and not of tradition, and religion by revelation to us, and not the history of theirs? The sun shines also today. Let us demand our own words and law and worship." His questions (which were also mine) had helped to shape, prophetically, this rather untraditional religious tradition.

It did not happen overnight, but in time that tradition became my own. Today I call it my chosen faith: Unitarian Universalism. In its midst I have found the support to keep alive the questions of the prophets, to be challenged in my moral and religious living. I have discovered a tradition that takes seriously the rights (and responsibilities) of the individual in ethical and religious matters, that recognizes that one of the sources of all effective moral faith is direct experience of transcendent mystery and wonder.

Each of us has transforming moments. Not all of them are soaring. Many are painful, breaking through our defenses to raise challenging questions of us, just as we so often have questions of life. In such moments, we can sometimes receive life once more as a gift, not a given. When we do, when we are more open to life's unfolding questions of us, then we can identify more deeply with others, with those who are also challenged. We can commit (or recommit) ourselves to join with them to serve justice, to love mercy, and to walk humbly together before the Mystery that gives us all life—and to do so even in the face of death.

Having made this noncreedal tradition my own, I still find that what I appreciate most within it are the individuals—including some long dead whose response to life's questions served to open the way for people like me. Among our prophets are Margaret Fuller, the pioneering advocate for women's rights and Emerson's friend; William Ellery Channing, the Unitarian minister who inspired both Fuller and Emerson; and John Murray, the founder of American Universalism, and his wife, Judith Sargent Murray. Their transforming experiences tell us much about this first source of our liberal faith.

Margaret Fuller was born in 1810 and was raised a Unitarian in Cambridge, Massachusetts. She was the eldest child of a father who doted on her, yet who was often away. He served twenty-four years in the U.S. Senate. "Tell Margaret I love her," the Senator wrote his wife, "if she learns to read." And she did. At her father's bidding, she got the kind of education then normally reserved for males—reading at the age of three, doing Latin at four, memorizing Vergil at five. As she later put it, her girlhood was steeped in the classics and shaped by "Roman virtues . . . by an earnest purpose, an indomitable will, by hardihood, self-command and force of expression."

By the time she reached thirteen, her outspoken opinions and independent manners began to shock New England parlor expectations of feminine reserve. Senator Fuller became alarmed. How would she ever find a husband? he asked Mrs. Fuller. Clearly, for her own good, their daughter's education would have to be reversed. So she was sent to the country, to Miss Prescott's School for Young Ladies. "My own world sank deep within," Margaret wrote, "away from the surface life . . . But my true life was only the dearer that it was secluded and veiled over . . . "

When she returned to Cambridge at the age of sixteen, Margaret Fuller became known as the most charming and interesting young woman in town. Young Harvard students came to her parlor to discuss Goethe and Schiller, Wordsworth and Coleridge. As a conversationalist, Fuller was truly brilliant. She knew how to listen, how to draw people out and help them refine their feelings and express their thoughts. She had "breadth and richness of culture," as one male friend said, "shown in her allusions or quotations, easy comprehension of new views, just discrimination, and truthfulness." She was also fun—full of "saucy spriteliness," a wit that extended to satire, and an intensity and self-assertion that seemed to attract and repell at once. Most young men were more than a little frightened of her.

With the political sweep of Andrew Jackson in 1828, Senator Fuller's political career came to an abrupt end. In a few years, he was dead. The family had by then retired to rural Massachusetts. There was little money; their mother was ill; one younger brother lost an eye; another died; a third was found to be retarded; and there were three others to tutor and tend. As the eldest daughter, Margaret Fuller "learned to rock a cradle, read a book, eat an apple and knit a stocking, all at the same time." She tried hard to keep in touch with friends writing letters. One Sunday she heard a minister friend preach on Goethe's favorite text: "Whatsoever thy hand findeth to do, do it with thy might." She began to write more intensely—letters, articles, a translation of Echermann's *Conversations with Goethe*. She even planned a biography of the German poet. But underneath her outward enthusiasm was a growing loneliness and depression.

Then one day Fuller had what can only be called a religious experience. She describes it in terms that sound more Buddhist than Christian: "I saw that there was no self; that selfishness was all folly, and the result of circumstance, that it was only because I thought the self real that I suffered; that I only had to live in the idea of the All and all was mine. This truth came to me, and I received it unhesitatingly; so that I was for that hour taken up into God." This was not some form of resignation. On the contrary, the experience

led to empowerment—to a deeper religious acceptance of life in both its joys and sorrows, and of herself as a vital part of the divine life.

"I accept the Universe!" she exclaimed. To which Emerson's friend Thomas Carlyle commented, "By gad, she'd better!" Fuller was often mistaken as some sort of egoist because she was not a conventional, demure, nineteenth-century woman. But what she was really saying Carlyle himself had said, that existence requires an "everlasting Yea," an affirmation stronger than all life's negations.

In the years that followed, Margaret Fuller became more self-confident. She became a member of Emerson's Transcendentalist circle, and editor of its publication, the *Dial*. In it she wrote the first major treatment of women's issues to be published in America, issued in book form as *Woman in the Nineteenth Century*. Her ability to identify with others had also been deepened. She led "conversations," educational sessions aimed at helping women express themselves and improve their self-image. Later, as a writer for Horace Greeley's *New York Tribune*, she became a pioneering investigative reporter, uncovering poor conditions in local asylums, jails, and other institutions. She also went to Europe as the *Tribune*'s first female foreign correspondent.

There, in 1848, she fell in love with a young Italian revolutionary, the Marchese d'Ossoli, who fought for

Garibaldi and the Roman Republic. Fuller ran a hospital and had their child, Angelino. In 1850, when the revolution collapsed, they decided to sail for New York. But their ship foundered off Fire Island and Margaret Fuller, her husband, and their infant son were all drowned. Fuller's body was never recovered. Yet the experience of this remarkable woman, who was true to herself against great odds, remained influential and inspired the lives of thousands of women and men. As she testified to her own and succeeding generations, "Cherish your best hopes as a faith, and abide by them in action."

Margaret Fuller was the product of a New England environment that was already thawing its rather chilly and restrictive Puritan culture. No one played a more central role in bringing a more humane spirit to New England theology than the Unitarian preacher William Ellery Channing.

Also the son of a public leader, Channing was born thirty years before Margaret Fuller, in 1780. His father served Newport, Rhode Island, both as district attorney and state attorney general. One day when Channing was still a young boy, his father took him with him to a public gathering. A huge crowd had assembled to hear a famous itinerant preacher. Years later Channing could still describe what he heard. The revivalist painted "a terrific picture of the lost condition of the human race rushing into hell . . . In very mov-

ing tones he besought his hearers to flee from the wrath to come into the arms of Jesus, who was described as wounded and bleeding at the hand of an inexorable God, who exacted from him the uttermost penalty due to a world of sinners."

At the end of the sermon, the boy was terrified as well as skeptical about the message. He submitted, however, when he heard his father say to a friend, "Sound doctrine that! Leaves no rag of self-righteousness to wrap the sinner in!" On the way home, he expected to hear solemn words on the family's plans for fleeing "the wrath to come." Yet all his father did was whistle! At supper, Mrs. Channing inquired whether the preacher had been a disappointment. "No," said her husband, "he's a strong man." Yet the evening passed quietly, without a word about escaping.

By bedtime, young Channing had an insight that led to questions. His father did not really believe the revivalist at all! Neither did most people. Did people really become better because of fear? He thought not. Was God really so harsh and cruel? Then why praise God in worship? Why did people say they believed one thing when their actions showed they believed something else? Is doctrine the most important thing in religion? or is it the way people live?

Years later, in a sermon dedicating a Unitarian church in his home town, Channing would say that the negative tone of religion during his boyhood had

been an "unhappy influence." His spirit had been renewed only by long walks on the beach. "There, in the sight of that beauty, in the sound of those waves . . . I poured out my thanksgiving and contrite confessions. There, in reverential sympathy with the mighty power around me, I became conscious of power within. There struggling thoughts and emotions broke forth, as if moved to utterance by nature's eloquence . . . "

As the minister of Boston's Federal Street Church, Channing eloquently preached what he called "practical religion"—the renewal of the spirit, intellectual integrity, and the application of one's moral insights and aspirations to daily living and social existence. He and other liberal ministers in the old Puritan congregations had ceased to require from those who wished to join the church creedal affirmations, evidence of personal conversion, or acceptance of doctrines such as predestination, vicarious atonement, or the Trinity. When this practice was denounced as heresy, as "unitarianism," Channing accepted the name, and began organizing, for mutual support, those who were similarly inclined.

Channing's ideal was an inclusive church—one from which no one could be excommunicated, except "by the death of goodness" in one's own breast. He became a leader in the movement away from a harsh and dogmatic Calvinism and toward a more liberal and lib-

erating theology. He preached grace, not fear, and spoke of human reason as a divine gift. Then he applied reason to religious life, with profound insight into human motivation, history, the Bible, and contemporary moral and social issues. He preached not retribution, but the love of God, and the human capacity for "likeness to God" in more divine living. He spoke of Jesus less as the second person of a metaphysical trinity than as a human example of human life lived to the fullness of its spiritual capacity.

His own character was widely revered. He inspired his parishioners, including such great souls as Dorothea Dix, the great crusader for more decent care for the mentally ill; Horace Mann, the promoter of free, universal public education; Samuel Gridley Howe, a pioneer in the education of the deaf and blind; and Julia Ward Howe, whose "Battle Hymn" represents the culmination of the long campaign Channing helped inspire for the abolition of American slavery. His influence was perhaps broader and deeper than any other American religious leader's in his time. Even today in Unitarian Universalist congregations his words about how to educate children continue to influence our church school programs:

The great end in religious instruction, is not to stamp our minds upon the young, but to stir up their own; not to make them see with our eyes, but to look

inquiringly and steadily with their own; not to give them a definite amount of knowledge, but to inspire a fervent love of truth; not to form an outward regularity, but to touch inward springs; not to bind them by ineradicable prejudices to our particular sect or peculiar notions, but to prepare them for impartial, conscientious judging of whatever subjects may be offered to their decision; not to burden the memory, but to quicken and strengthen the power of thought; not to impose religion upon them in the form of arbitrary rules, but to awaken the conscience, the moral discernment. In a word, the great end is to awaken the soul; to bring understanding, conscience and heart into earnest vigorous action on religious and moral truth, to excite and cherish spiritual life.

Unitarians were not alone in bringing a more humane spirit to religion in the late eighteenth and early nineteenth centuries. In 1770, ten years before Channing was born, a man named John Murray came to America. He was to become the founder of the other side of our denominational family, American Universalism.

Standard Christian theology divides the saved from the damned. But universalism is the teaching that ultimately God will save all souls: universal salvation. It finds the notion of permanent damnation to an everlasting hell incompatible with faith in a loving

God. In the history of theology this doctrine can be traced back to Origen of Alexandria, a second-century theologian. But in American history, it denotes a distinctive religious movement, one that began independently of the Unitarians and had a remarkable influence through the nineteenth century. Universalism nurtured a broad range of remarkable women and men, including some of the first women ministers of any denomination. Then, in the 1960s, the movement merged with the Unitarians to form today's Unitarian Universalist Association.

"Give the people . . . something of your vision," said John Murray to his fellow Universalists. "You may possess only a small light, but uncover it, let it shine, use it in order to bring more light and understanding to the hearts and minds of men and women. Do not preach so as to deepen their theological despair. Give them not hell, but hope and courage."

He knew from his own experience about the need for both. Converted to universalist thought among eighteenth-century English Methodists, Murray experienced rejection as a preacher. While caring for his dying young wife, he fell into debt and later spent time in debtor's prison. In 1770 he left England to make a new start in America. He had sworn off preaching. But his ship went aground on the New Jersey coast. Sent ashore for supplies, he was helped by a farmer, Thomas Potter, who had built a chapel and

set it aside, open to all existing sects, but awaiting a more inclusive and hopeful preaching of the Gospel. Potter told Murray that his message was more needed and welcome on this side of the ocean, and predicted that his ship would not be able to sail again until he preached it!

Potter was right on both counts. Standing in the pulpit of that little New Jersey chapel, Murray discovered that ordinary Americans were receptive to his message. The establishment religion was Calvinist. God had predestined some to prosperity, others to labor; some to ease, others to pain; some to fame, others to obscurity; some to salvation, others to be damned. Many people fatalistically accepted Calvinism. But others were hungry to hear preachers like Murray expound his favorite text: "God has not destined us for wrath, but for salvation" (1 Thess. 5:9).

Judith Sargent, a young widow of literary talent and aspiration, heard him and in 1788 they were married. By that time Murray was already notorious as an unorthodox minister who challenged the religious establishment where it hurt—in the pocketbook. He had led the congregation he gathered in Gloucester, Massachusetts, which included his wife's parents, in a lawsuit. They had challenged the right of the town to tax them for support of the local parish church and its ministry. And they had won, striking an important early blow for the separation of church and state.

Judith Sargent Murray was also an independent soul and spiritually nourished more by direct experience of life's transcending mystery and wonder than by social or religious convention. She wrote poetry, plays, and essays such as "The Equality of the Sexes." Secretly, as she once confided in her journal, she wanted to "descend with celebrity to posterity" through her writing. But she realized how the writings of women were then dismissed by most people, so she wrote anonymously or under various male pseudonyms. In that guise she was frequently published in the best journals. It's said that her husband once began to read aloud to her an essay he admired. After a time, through some allusion, he realized the brilliant author could be none other than his wife! The three volumes of her collected writings, *The Gleaner*, show that she anticipated nearly all the later arguments for women's rights.

Judith Sargent Murray remains little known, while Margaret Fuller achieved an enduring reputation. In comparison with the more prominent and literary Unitarians, most early Universalists lived and died rather obscurely. Many Unitarians were public leaders, Harvard-educated (or the equivalent), and of merchant class or professional background. The Universalists were more often ordinary fisherfolk, artisans, shopkeepers, and farmers. Among the few Universalists who received widespread recognition in the nineteenth century was the New York editor Horace Greeley.

"Go west, young man," said Greeley, "Go west!" As America did so, its Calvinist heritage went along, too, expressing itself in frontier revivals. But the Universalists, with their gospel of reassurance, of God's love, went along as well. Evangelical and progressive, they reached people in rural hamlets and small towns. Some congregations were fragile and closed as rural hamlets disappeared or revivalism moderated. But others survived and can be found today from Caribou, Maine, and Canon, Georgia, to Pasadena and Santa Paula, California. [The Universalist Church of America merged with the American Unitarian Association, in 1961, to form the Unitarian Universalist Association, but the Universalist heritage remains a vital part of our inclusive faith.]

The difference between the two sides of our denominational family was once summarized by a minister who knew both Universalist and Unitarian congregations. Thomas Starr King grew up a Massachusetts Universalist, then became the pastor of the First Unitarian Church in San Francisco as the Civil War was beginning. He is credited for "saving California for the Union," and the Unitarian Universalist seminary in Berkeley is named for him. "The Universalists believe that God is too good to damn them," said Starr King, "whereas the Unitarians believe they are too good to be damned!" And indeed our Universalist heritage continues to challenge the Unitarian tendency to

be "fit but few." We are challenged to reach out to all sorts and conditions of people, to be open to the individual character of all human religious experience.

A friend of mine once wrote a historical novel set in the American West of the nineteenth century. In it, a young man is asked about religion. "I ain't got no experience," he replies. What he means, of course, is that he has not converted; he has not confessed his sinful nature, given his heart to Jesus, or come forward at a revival meeting. But as the story develops, he (along with the country) grows and changes, and his reply becomes more and more ironic. The point is we *all* have experience, but our experience may not always fit conventional or expected religious patterns.

"I'm not religious," people sometimes claim. "Then tell me about your experience," I say in return. We may not be conventionally pious, but we all experience life, and there are religious dimensions to explore within that experience. Emerson knew this. After having lost his father at the age of nine and suffering the death of his five-year-old son, he wrote "Experience," the most sad but most profound essay he ever wrote. "We wake," he said, "and find ourselves on a stair; there are stairs below us which we seem to have ascended; there are stairs above us, many a one, which go upward and out of sight."

As hinted at in this brief passage and demonstrated throughout his life and writings, Emerson's response

to the mystery of life and presence of death was, if not conventionally, profoundly religious. Based not on revelation, but on his own difficult experiences, Emerson discovered within himself and yet transcending him, something deeper and higher than his grief. He discovered it not on a ladder to heaven, but on earthly stairs, representing a sense of indebtedness to those who have preceded us and of obligation to those who will come after we are gone. Yet the renewal, the affirmation, the wonder at being alive, can only come in the present, while we have time to be amazed and grateful.

I make the same point to those who tell me, "I don't believe in God." "Tell me about the God that you don't believe in," I often reply. "The chances are that I don't believe in 'Him' either." I believe, as Dag Hammarskjöld did, that "God does not die on the day when we cease to believe in a personal deity. But we die on the day when our lives cease to be illuminated by the steady radiance, renewed daily, of a wonder, the source of which is beyond all reason." Similarly, Emerson said, "It is not what we believe, but the universal impulse to believe . . . that is the principal fact." Through our own direct experience we too may discover a profound sense of wonder about the gift of life and be led to gratitude, renewal of the spirit, and openness to the forces that create and uphold life.

"Belief is many things," said one of our modern leaders, A. Powell Davies, "and so is disbelief. But religion is something that happens to you when you open your mind to truth, your conscience to justice, and your heart to love." In Unitarian Universalist congregations we do not try to make one another fit a given pattern of experience. But we do discover together that there are religious dimensions in all our varied human experience.

For us, religious experience is direct and personal. It may be joyous—a transformative moment of awakening like being present at a child's birth. Or it may be as painful as the birth itself or as wrenching as grief. Sometimes it takes something very close to our own death, or the death of someone we love, to break through our usual defenses and remind us what a gift it is to be alive and to be able to love. Part of all authentic experience is deeply inward—beginning to trust what Channing called "the power of God within." But often it is dependent upon the agency of others whose insight, courage, or love helps expand our idea of what human life can be.

This is why Unitarian Universalists choose to gather in religious communities, where other individuals and, yes, a whole tradition, help us to keep heart and conscience and mind receptive. In our churches and fellowships we are constantly invited to "accept the

Universe," to emphasize "practical religion," to give the world "not hell, but hope and courage." I discovered this way to wonder and spiritual renewal nearly a quarter century ago, and shall always be grateful. Not only is my religion grounded in my own direct experience, but it is also sustained by the experience of others. Like Judith Sargent Murray, I may not "descend with celebrity to posterity," but I do hope to make the world a bit better for those who come after me. With her and with Emerson, you and I share this human experience: we are on the stairs.

PART 2

Words and deeds of prophetic women and men which challenge us to confront powers and structures of evil with justice, compassion, and the transforming power of love.

3

Deeds Not Creeds

Forrest Church

I have an almost complete disregard of precedent and a faith
in the possibility of something better. It irritates me to be
told how things always have been done . . . I defy the tyranny of precedent. I cannot afford the luxury of a closed
mind. I go for anything new that might improve the past.
            —Clara Barton, Universalist layperson
            and founder of the American Red Cross

We are a liberal church community which has not only
dared to preach freedom but to live in freedom as well,
which has not only prophesied a more just day to come but
has dared to live prophetically right now.
            —Mark Belletini, Unitarian Universalist minister

SINCE THE FIRST CENTURY, a debate has continued
within the Christian community concerning whether
salvation can best be secured by faith or by works.
Even when Unitarianism and Universalism identified
themselves exclusively as part of the Christian community, both leaned in the direction of works. Such

Be ye doers of the word, and
Faith without works is dead"
our liberal faith.

that both denominations that
an Universalism are named after
minations are known according
y or organization. For instance,
ipreme authority to their bishops,
ir presbyters or elders, and Con-
gregatio... ch congregation—Unitarian Universalists are congregational in polity, but this is not
reflected in our name. Other denominations refer to
themselves according to some specific practice (Baptists
and Seventh Day Adventists); theological approach
(Methodists and Christian Scientists); founder (Lutherans and Swedenborgians); or fidelity to God (Disciples of Christ and Jehovah's Witnesses). The Catholic
church claims universalism—that is what "catholic"
means—but not in the doctrinal sense of the word.
Our communions, however, are named after doctrines.
Unitarianism refers to a belief in the unity of God,
distinguishing early Unitarians from trinitarians; and
Universalism affirms salvation for all people. The two
come together to form the most doctrinally free of all
denominations which, ironically, has two doctrines in
its name.

Part of the reason for this paradox is that others
named us. In the early nineteenth century we were

accused by orthodox Christians of the heresies of universalism and unitarianism. Perhaps we chose the names that others gave us because they indicate the expansiveness of our faith. For if there is one God (truth or reality) for all, and if we all have equal access to this, regardless of the specifics of our respective faiths, the only thing that differentiates one person's righteousness from that of another is reflected in his or her deeds.

Here we have to be careful, however. Doctrinally, Universalism's principal theological contribution lies in striking hell from the theological menu. Complementing this, Unitarianism (in addition to affirming God's oneness) removed original sin. Together, they conspired brilliantly on behalf of goodness. The problem is that even as a theology based upon evil and sinfulness tends to stint on goodness, one based upon goodness may be equally obtuse when it comes to evil and sin. Too much mercy can squeeze out justice; and too much attention to our better nature can blind us to the awesome human capacity for evil.

In this country, our churches were established in the nineteenth century as an alternative to hard-bitten Calvinism (the faith of our Puritan forebears), which claimed not only that all of us were born into sin, but also that some of us were born to be saved and others to be damned. The rubric for this is double predestination. If we were born to be damned, there was nothing we could do; if we were born to be saved, we would cash in our tickets simply by announcing our fidelity to Christ. Double predestination was a logical conclusion drawn from one of the basic premises of Christian theology: God's omniscience. If God knows everything, including everything that is going to happen in each of our lives, then it stands to reason that God knows—from the very moment we are born—whether we will go to Heaven or to Hell.

In the early nineteenth century, both Unitarians and Universalists rebelled against this sort of purblind determinism. Sin became a dirty word in Unitarian and Universalist circles. Liberal theologians responded by claiming that we were born good. Any evils that manifested themselves during the course of our lives were the fault of environment, education, lack of opportunity, poor nurture, bad example, or discrimination. These were the things that led us to fall, not sin.

Placed in the context of today's debate, Calvinists attributed our fate to genetics, liberals to environment. The weakness of the Calvinist argument is not that it was based upon original sin, but that it involved a capricious resolution of some people's sin by divine orchestration, while others were left hopeless, swinging in the wind. But, in rebelling against this blasphemy against the creator and the creation, we liberals went too far in the opposite direction. We concluded that sin was not a genetic predisposition, but rather an imposition by society upon children born not sinful, but pure and good.

Having observed my own children, I am ambivalent when it comes to these two positions, nature and nurture. We are born with a capacity for both good and evil, and society contributes directly to the development of our aptitude for each. Einstein once said that God does not throw dice. I disagree. That is precisely what "God" does. Each fertilized egg is a throw of the dice, and so is the family, environment, nation, century, and set of opportunities—or lack thereof—into which we are born.

Since we have no control over our birth, original sin, coupled with double predestination, is not a particularly constructive concept. The first Unitarians and Universalists rejected it for this reason. They knew that, regardless of our circumstances at birth, with help and effort most of us are capable of making a positive difference in our own lives and the life of our times. But, as common sense reminds us, we are also capable of the opposite—even the best of us are.

In 1858 the essayist, George Templeton Strong, and his wife, Ellie, attended one of Henry Whitney Bellows' lectures on social issues. Bellows served as minister of All Souls Church in New York for forty-three years. A great institutionalist, he is credited for building a coherent denomination out of an idiosyncratic collection of Unitarian churches. Strong wrote about our illustrious predecessor in his diary.

He blew well; his lecture was pleasant and instructive, but it is very curious to observe the unpracticality of all sermons, essays, and lectures by men of Bellows' school, Yankee-Unitarianism, when they undertake any practical subject. . . . They are sensible, plausible, candid, subtle, and original in discussing any social evil or abuse. But somehow they don't get *at* it. You feel that you have heard or read a very clever and entertaining paper, embodying a good deal of clear and deep thought, and you ask, "What shall I do?" and pause for a reply, and pause in vain. If you get a reply that seems definite, it is generally resolvable by analysis into some formula like "Lift yourself up by the waistband of your own breeches." "Move your limbs only once and your dead palsy will be cured." Convince your "dangerous classes" that honesty is the best policy, and they will become useful citizens. But Bellows is far sounder and wiser than the great majority of his school. Its defects are mitigated in him by his native common sense which is strong enough to neutralize a good deal of his Unitarianism.

The Unitarianism that Strong is disparaging here is

a perceived tendency by those who believe in the goodness of humanity to refuse to face up to the reality and consequence of evil. The warning is worth our attention, for every principle, if exaggerated, is responsible for its own undoing. Yet, even as Strong was critiquing Henry Whitney Bellows, Bellows was emerging as one of the most active and effective humanitarians of his generation. In the early 1860s, as founder and president of the American Sanitary Commission (the precursor of the American Red Cross), he and his cohorts raised six million dollars, an astounding sum in the mid nineteenth century, and built an organization that eased the suffering of the wounded and dying on both sides during the Civil War.

This task was accomplished with the cooperation of Unitarian and Universalist laypeople throughout the country. Mary Ashton Rice Livermore, a Universalist, organized a fair in Chicago that raised seventy thousand dollars for the cause. Livermore oversaw the entire operation, selecting supplies, supervising transportation and distribution, and attending to a prudent disbursement of funds. In later years, steeled by her success (achieved despite considerable odds, including the unwillingness of many men in Chicago to take her seriously), Livermore moved to Massachusetts, led the Massachusetts Suffrage Association, and founded *The Agitator,* a paper devoted to suffrage and women's rights. Devoting her life to "the work of making the law and justice synonymous for women," Mary Livermore demonstrated her faith through works.

Bellows and Livermore, one a Unitarian minister, the other a Universalist laywoman, persuasively counter Strong's critique of the ineffectuality of religious liberalism. And they are but two of a great cloud of nineteenth-century Unitarian and Universalist witnesses. People such as Clara Barton (health care), Henry Bergh (animal rights), Adin Ballou (industrial policy), and Susan B. Anthony (women's rights) served in the front ranks of the great humanitarian movements of their day. These were indeed prophetic women and men whose words and deeds challenge us to confront powers and structures of evil with justice, compassion, and the transforming power of love.

Theodore Parker is another eloquent witness. The most popular preacher in Boston, Parker wrote his sermons with a pistol by his side, not to protect himself, but, should the need arise, to defend escaped slaves traveling on the underground railroad toward Canada. Parker sharpened the cutting edge of every major social justice issue of his day. His fellow ministers in Boston, even Unitarian ministers, shunned him, but Parker was far from daunted. In 1854 he went so far as to lead a crowd of vigilantes on an unsuccessful attempt to storm the local courthouse and free Anthony Burns, a fugitive slave. "Freedom is worth nothing in a country that condones slavery," he declaimed, adding with a smile, "I'm the most hated man in America."

The words of such activists as Parker and Bellows, Barton and Livermore, rang true to the authenticity of their deeds. They knew, as Thomas Jefferson once said, that "it is in our lives, and not our words that our religion must be read." Yet Strong's critique is still worth pondering. As both Parker and Bellows remind us, it is one thing to have the right sentiments, and something else again to act upon them. Without the proof of deeds, good intentions and right opinions are nothing more than empty shells. "Freedom, whether political or religious, has no power to produce anything," Bellows preached. "It merely leaves the faculties free to act."

As Mary Livermore or Theodore Parker could have told us, morality and moralism are very different things. In fact, they run at cross purposes. Moral posturing gives us a sense of accomplishment without our having actually done anything. In short, we feel that we have washed our hands every time we wring them. It's like a mock purification ceremony which gives only the appearance of cleansing.

Take our response to the religious right. It does not really matter what we may think of the politics or the religion of our fundamentalist neighbors. All that matters is whether we are willing to live up to the promise and power of our own faith. Morality not proved in deeds is always betrayed by words, however right-minded, lofty, and sage. I call this sin.

Though far from exclusive to Unitarian Universalists, the principal sin besetting many of us today is the sin of sophisticated resignation. This sin is particularly insidious because it comes with its own veil. That is, it appears respectable. It allows us to feel strongly about injustices without prompting us to do anything about them. This sin is tailor-made for many of us because it is fed by knowledge. We know so much about the world's problems, and their enormity, that however much we want to do about them, we feel impotent. What could we do to affect hunger, homelessness, AIDS, or the threat of nuclear annihilation? How much easier it is to watch our diets and tone our bodies. For many of us, self-improvement (both physical and spiritual) has displaced the transformation of society as our principal moral concern.

Not so the religious right! Even those among them who so fervently believe that the end of the world is imminent are not sitting on their hands waiting. They are organizing themselves to beat the band, to beat the devil in fact, all the way to kingdom come.

Our heritage reminds us that we are a faith of deeds not creeds. According to the second of our faith's five sources, "words and deeds of prophetic women and men which challenge us to confront powers and structures of evil with justice, compassion, and the transforming power of love," we can be proud of many of our Unitarian and Universalist forbears who did precisely that. But what about us? What does this pride of identity avail us, if the extent of our own moral exercise (in addition to jogging) is limited to clucking our tongues, throwing up our hands, and—when we do finally act—issuing an occasional smug and ineffectual manifesto? The answer is absolutely nothing. Right-wing fundamentalists marshall far more energy, money, and talent to advance their narrow creed, than we do to transform the world according to our own Unitarian and Universalist vision. Our slogan, "deeds not creeds," thus becomes a mockery. Too often we have neither, while they have both.

In face of this, we are left with two choices. One is to climb off our moral high horse; the other is to learn how to ride. Both are preferable to high-minded posturing and sophisticated resignation, but only the latter represents the promise and fulfillment of our faith.

Fortunately, though the flame of true, as opposed to mock, prophecy may at times seem to flicker, even in recent history there are beacons illuminating the darkness to help us find our way. I think of the First Unitarian Church in Los Angeles, where worship services were simulcast in English, Korean, and Spanish, encouraging the development of a richly diverse multiethnic community. And I think of the Universalist meetinghouse in Provincetown, Massachusetts, where special outreach to the gay and lesbian community has transformed a once sleepy parish into the hub of town life and activity. There are many such stories, but I close this chapter with one that is particularly striking, taken from the recent history of All Souls Unitarian Church in Washington, D.C.

A. Powell Davies was one of the most effective Unitarian evangelists in this century. During his twelve-year tenure in the late 1940s and early 1950s as minister of All Souls, Davies sponsored the establishment of eleven new Unitarian societies, while routinely preaching to a thousand people or more in his own church (including such social prophets as Adlai Stevenson, Senator Paul Douglas, and Justice William O. Douglas, who edited Davies' writings shortly after his death). There is no doubt part of his success was due to personal magnetism, but he also had a vision for transforming society according to the principles of justice, compassion, and love.

Davies did not only preach against segregation. One Sunday morning he called for a boycott of all Washington restaurants that served only whites. Enlisting his congregation, and tweaking the conscience of the editorial board of *The Washington Post,* within weeks Davies had won the day. Where high platitudes would surely have worked little suasion, the social and economic pressures triggered by his action soon took their noble toll. Through Davies' efforts, and those of his congregation, at long last the restaurants of Washington were open to all.

This spirit is infectious. In 1959, two years after Davies died, the Reverend James Reeb came to Washington to assist Davies' successor, Duncan Howlett, as a member of the All Souls' ministerial staff. Soon radicalized by the poverty surrounding the church, Reeb determined to devote his life to social service on behalf of the poor. He and his family moved to Boston, where he worked first in an open ministry, and then with the Quakers, to facilitate the development of low-cost housing.

In 1965, Reeb's growing commitment to and involvement in the civil rights movement impelled him to join the marchers in Selma, Alabama. There, at dusk one evening, while leaving a restaurant in a black neighborhood in the company of two Unitarian Universalist ministers, Orloff Miller and Clark Olsen, Reeb and his companions were accosted by four white men wielding baseball bats. Miller and Olsen were beaten but survived; James Reeb was murdered.

In his very first sermon to the congregation of All Souls, Reeb asked, "Is there nothing worth risking one's life for? Are there no dreams or goals so important that we risk our own destruction to gain them?" He answered these questions with his life.

In the early 1970s, powered by the conviction that a racially mixed church in an all-black neighborhood should have a black senior minister, Duncan Howlett (who was also Reeb's biographer) resigned from the All Souls pulpit. Today, under the leadership of Daniel Webster Aldridge, Jr., All Souls' second black senior minister, this historic congregation continues eloquently to witness to the prophetic promise of our liberal faith.

Still it must be said, although Unitarian Universalists were prominent in the struggle for civil rights (with some filling key positions of leadership, such as Whitney Young—a member of both the Unitarian Universalist Church of Atlanta, and the Community Unitarian Church in White Plains, New York, and trustee of the Unitarian Universalist Service Committee) when judged according to the spirit of the second of our five sources of faith, our record is spotty. From its inception, Unitarian Universalism has been and remains predominantly a white, upper-middle-class denomination. Those most vulnerable to injustice in our society—the poor and people of color—have every reason to say of us, as George Templeton Strong once said of many nineteenth-century Unitarians: "They are sensible, plausible, candid, subtle, and original in discussing any social evil or abuse. But somehow they don't get *at* it." In short, our hands will not be clean until we get them dirty, until we roll up our sleeves and match our words with deeds.

Fortunately, as all Universalists know, we sinners were born to be saved. So long as people like Henry

Whitney Bellows, Mary Livermore, Theodore Parker, Clara Barton, A. Powell Davies, Whitney Young, and James Reeb continue to confront the "powers and structures of evil with justice, compassion, and the transforming power of love," we shall be challenged to grow in service and in faith.

4

The Known and the Unknown

John A. Buehrens

Who are these Unitarian Universalists, standing around the coffee table on Sunday morning discussing last night's movie and next fall's election; reviewing the morning sermon, designing tomorrow's education, storming over next century's oceans? Joyful celebrants of the gift of life, mixing nonsense with the quest of the ages, turning secular need into concerned action, serving wine on the lawn and petitions in the foyer?

> —*Betty Mills, Unitarian Universalist layperson*

Keepers of the dream will come again and again, from what humble places we do not know, to struggle against the crushing odds, leaving behind no worldly kingdom, but only a gleam in the dark hills to show how high we may climb. Already there have been many such heroes—women and men whose names we do not know, but whose words and deeds still light the path for us.

> —*H. G. Wenzel, Unitarian Universalist layperson*

IN THE MOVIE *Oh God!* George Burns plays the title role. "Was Jesus your son?" he is asked. "Of course Jesus was my son," he replies, taking a pull on his cigar. "But so were Confucius, the Buddha, Mohammed . . . and a lot of other guys who didn't get such good publicity." He neglects to claim any daughters. More poor publicity.

Robert Raible, minister of our church in Dallas for many years, used to close his public prayers by saying, "We ask these things in the names of all those, known and unknown, remembered and forgotten, who lived and died as true servants of humankind. Amen." Bible-belt folks, used to hearing "in Jesus' name we pray" (even when Jews and other non-Christians were present) would have their consciousness gently expanded. His point was this: Prophetic and challenging words and deeds are not the sole possession of one exemplar long ago, or even of the more famous recent heroes and heroines of humankind. If that were so there would be little hope for the rest of us, though we do not presume to be great prophets or aspire to heroics. We only hope to live, as Lincoln said, "with faithfulness to the right as God gives us to see the right."

Every religious movement has its martyrs and heroes, of course. Unitarian Universalism is no exception. We have already mentioned some famous Americans associated with our free faith. But our heritage also goes deeper—back to Europe, to those lesser known radicals of the Reformation who pioneered an approach to religion emphasizing freedom, reason, and tolerance. Some of them also deserve to be better remembered.

There was, for example, King John Sigismund of Transylvania (1540–71), the only Unitarian king in history. Reigning in a time of strident theological debate among Catholics, Lutherans, Calvinists, and Unitarians, he issued the first public decree of religious toleration. The leading advocate for the Unitarians in his realm was Francis David, who as the Reformation had progressed had gone from being a Franciscan Catholic to a Lutheran, then a Calvinist, and finally to believing in the unity of God. At a debate sponsored by the king, David's opponents—each with a past claim on his soul—declared that if victorious, they would see him condemned to death as an apostate and heretic. David replied, in the truest spirit of our faith, "If I win, I shall defend to the death your right to be wrong." King John Sigismund made him court chaplain. Both believed that pluralism in faith need not mean civic and moral disorder. In David's words, "We need not think alike to love alike."

But most people in the sixteenth century did not believe that. To have firm but unconventional beliefs could mean paying with one's life. Michael Servetus (1511–53), for example, was a devout Spaniard, with both medical and legal training, who came of age as both Reformers and Catholic humanists were discussing the true basis for Christianity. He found certain formulations of traditional trinitarian dogma to be troublesome, and said so, claiming that as an abstract doctrine belief in the Trinity was the wrong test for authentic religion. To Muslims and Jews (of whom a Spaniard could not help but be conscious) it was a stumbling block. Besides, scholars were showing that the Trinity was not a New Testament doctrine, but one imposed much later by church councils and Christian emperors who wanted a uniform dogma and creed. Servetus's book, *On the Errors of the Trinity* (1531), disturbed both Catholic and Protestant leaders. The Inquisition hunted him, but for two decades he escaped. Living in France under a false name, Servetus practiced medicine and even contributed to scientific history by writing a pioneering treatise on the blood's circulation. Finally, he went to Calvin's Geneva to press his argument with the Reformers. Captured, tried, and refusing to recant, he was burned at the stake as a heretic on 27 October 1553. His death became a *cause célèbre,* igniting throughout Europe a broad debate about tolerance, reason, and the voluntary principle in religion.

Michael Servetus thus became relatively known. But others in those years who had the same convictions remain almost forgotten. Katherine Vogel (or Weigel) lived in Krakow, Poland. As early as the 1520s, when the Reformation was first stirring in southern Poland, she was reported to the bishop as a heretic. It may be that she had been influenced by the monotheism of her Jewish friends, but in any case she freely confessed that she did not believe in the Trinity, only in the unity of God. Jesus had believed no differently, she declared. The bishop reacted by locking her in a chapel of the city's principal church to make her recant. He kept her there for ten years. Finally, on 19 April 1539, she was led out to the square, still obdurate. And, witnesses say, the white-haired woman of eighty went "boldly and cheerfully." Her last words echoed those of Socrates, testifying that neither in this life or the next can anything evil befall the soul of one who stands loyal to the truth as one is given to know it. Then she too was burned at the stake.

A few years ago, I visited a memorial near the site where Servetus died. Overlooking a hospital, the rough stone carries an inscription saying it was erected "by the spiritual heirs of John Calvin" and that a great wrong was committed in the case of Servetus; the gospel can only be preached authentically where freedom of conscience is respected. In Krakow, however, I found no plaque in memory of Katherine Vogel.

It is not just the celebrated martyrs and heroes who help to redeem this world, who confront "the powers and structures of evil with justice, compassion, and the transforming power of love." Even today, the difficult, ordinary heroism of unknown people in their daily lives is often more important than the inspiring words of their better-known leaders. While I was in Krakow, for example, Polish Solidarity leader Lech Walesa received yet another award. But what impressed me most in Poland was the sight of ordinary people taking daily risks to extend freedom, justice, and human dignity. I saw old people, young people, and even children filing past soldiers to put flowers on an improvised memorial to Father Popieluszko, the Solidarity supporter whom the secret police had kidnapped, then killed. Every few weeks, I was told, the army would dismantle the memorial, but the people would rebuild it—if need be, in a different place.

It is often said that totalitarian governments cannot be effectively confronted by nonviolent methods. But I saw people using such methods, not to gain power, but to assert most effectively their inalienable rights to freedom of conscience, of expression, and of association. Watching them, I thought of other "ordinary" people—those in America who marched at Selma, or "sat in" to desegregate lunch counters; those who fought for our national independence, or who won for women the right to vote; those who even now fight against AIDS and bigotry, strive for peace, speak for the voiceless, defend the environment.

I also thought of Poland's almost forgotten but once flourishing Unitarian movement. In the late 1500s and early 1600s, Poland enjoyed a degree of religious pluralism and toleration it has not known since. Several hundred thousand members of the Protestant reformed church held unitarian beliefs. Their spiritual leader was an Italian by birth, a humanist named Faustus Sozzini (or Socinus). A biblical scholar, Socinus believed theologians had made a terrible mistake in agreeing with Greek philosophers that God is not affected or changed by what we do (or fail to do) here on earth.

In 1658, under the influence of the Counter-Reformation, the Polish Parliament took aim at nontrinitarians by decreeing that those who would not profess belief in the Trinity could not be landowners, or have full civic and political rights. Some fled to Transylvania; others stayed. But gradually the Polish Socinians were reduced in number. By World War II the last of them perished in the Holocaust. Even the Socinian monuments and churches had by then all been obliterated. Today, only the grave of Socinus has been restored. When I placed some flowers there as I had at Auschwitz, I told myself that God must have been affected by the persecution and death of so many people—must have wept, and not forgotten.

Being in Poland also reminded me of what the great Jewish theologian Martin Buber taught about the character of the modern world. In the beginning, he said, at the time of the French Revolution, *liberty, equality,* and *fraternity* (what might better be called the *kinship of all*) became the hallowed ideals of modern Europe. But after further revolutions in the West and East, the three diverged. Liberty went west, to America. But along the way its character changed. It became the freedom to exploit, to squander, to dissipate. Equality went east, to the Soviet Union and later to China. It too degenerated, becoming the submergence of the individual in a faceless collective—at its worst, the equality of the Gulag or that of the Red Guards.

Today, Buber observed, there are people in the West, such as Martin Luther King, who are struggling to reunite liberty with equality, at least equality of opportunity. And there are people in the East, such as Lech Walesa, who are struggling to return equality to a companionship with liberty. But neither effort can ever progress, much less succeed, Buber warned, unless we remember the missing element, human kinship. This is the religious element. It alone can bind together the other two. It reminds us that we are all sisters and brothers on this earth, children of one great mystery. Kinship can be recovered only by modern prophets who respect ordinary people, who will nurture, rather than exploit, their hopes and faith; by humble prophets who will dare to proclaim "the prophethood of all believers."

The person who coined that phrase was a contemporary Unitarian Universalist, the late James Luther Adams—often called among us "the Smiling Prophet."

It was a well-earned appellation, bestowed on a man of great moral realism and spiritual vibrancy. As a teacher of religious ethics for over half a century, Adams called on religious liberals to go beyond the Protestant principle of the "priesthood of all believers" and to test our "prophethood" by voluntarily coming together to serve a renewed vision of liberty, equality, and human kinship. As this master of aphorism and anecdote told ministerial students for two generations at the universities of Chicago and Harvard, "by their *groups* shall ye know them."

Raised a fundamentalist in the Pacific Northwest, Adams met secular modernity in Minnesota, at college. His period of disdain for religion was brief, however. A wise professor helped him realize that of all careers, the one that came most naturally to him was preacher—though his religious ideas were unorthodox and idealistic. Adams then went to Harvard where he became a Unitarian. As minister of our church in Salem, Massachusetts, in the 1920s, he played a leading role in reconciliation between striking mill workers and factory owners. But the theological roots of his social ethics were not clarified until the 1930s when he went to Germany to study and prepare for seminary teaching.

In Germany he saw the Nazis get little opposition from vague idealists. In fact, he saw many be seduced by the Nazis' talk of health, nature, "folk" and pre-

Christian religious inspiration. On the other hand, he witnessed the underground "Confessing Church," which was made up of those Christians who dared to resist Nazi ideology and anti-Semitism. Adams met and worked with the underground leaders. In this crucible, his faith became firmly, irrevocably cast in the pattern of the biblical prophets, with their eternal hostility toward all idolatries of blood and soil.

One story about Adams may serve to illustrate how modern Unitarian Universalists still find their faith rooted in the prophetic tradition. In the 1950s, while teaching in Chicago, Adams served on the board of the First Unitarian Church. The minister had already been outspoken about local issues of racial justice. One night, at a meeting from which the minister was absent, one of the trustees began to complain, suggesting that this was politics, not religion, from the pulpit; that it was alienating people, including him and his wife; and that both the minister and church should be "more realistic." When he lapsed into racial slurs, his fellow trustees, including Adams, interrupted.

"What is the purpose of a church?" they asked. Did he want the church only to make people comfortable? only to confirm them in their prejudices and not morally challenge them?

"Well, no," the so-called "realist" admitted.

"Then what *is* the purpose of a church?" the others kept asking.

"How should I know?" the man said, "I'm no theologian."

"But you're a member here, and a trustee of this church," said Adams and the others, refusing to let him off the hook.

As Adams told the story, the discussion continued until about one o'clock when fatigue combined with the Holy Spirit and the man blurted out, "Well, I guess the purpose of a church is, uh, to get hold of people like me, and to change 'em."

One trustee of evangelical background suggested that before they adjourn they rise and sing together "Amazing grace! how sweet the sound . . . I once was lost but now am found, was blind but now I see."

Who are these modern Unitarian Universalists standing around the coffee table discussing race relations, AIDS, last night's movie, and next fall's election? They may not all be prophets. They almost certainly won't all predict the election correctly. They won't even all agree about the candidates, or about the movie. They won't all be faithful unto death like Katherine Vogel or Francis David, though they will affirm that "we need not think alike to love alike." And they will express that love by caring about the world around them, discussing ideas, struggling together so as not to be solo prophets, but a prophetic, Spirit-led community—one in which as Adams said, "people think and work together to interpret the signs of the times in the light of their faith, to make explicit the epochal thinking which the times demand. The prophetic liberal church is the church in which all members share the common responsibility to attempt to foresee the consequences of human behavior, both individual and institutional, with the intention of making history instead of merely being pushed around by it. Only through the 'prophethood' of all believers can we foresee doom and mend our common ways."

In many religious movements nearly all religious and moral authority is vested in the founders, or in their present representatives, the ordained clergy. But that is not so in Unitarian Universalism. Our larger congregations usually prefer, when possible, to have the professional services of both ordained parish ministers and ministers of religious education. But each congregation chooses its own ministers through a search committee and congregational vote. No hierarchy can impinge on local autonomy, or do more than recommend available clergy through accepted procedures. And other, usually smaller, Unitarian Universalist groups organize themselves without any resident minister at all. Laypeople conduct the Sunday service, supply the pulpit, and witness to our values in their local community. For instance, the "chaplains" in our Canadian congregations are laypeople trained and allowed by civil law to perform rites of passage such as the dedication of children, weddings, and memorial services. Many fellowships (as most such lay-led congregations are called) were founded under a denominational extension program headed, in the late forties and through the fifties, by lay leader Monroe Husbands. They illustrate quite graphically how the principle of the priesthood and prophethood of all is valued throughout our religious movement. Whether served by an ordained minister or not, each of our local congregations draws up its own bylaws, has its own, lay-led governance, supports its programs and staff with members' contributions, and operates according to democratic principles.

The democratic emphasis in our religion is rooted, again, in the heritage of the biblical prophets. Adams was fond of the story in the book of Numbers when Moses is warned that two men named Eldad and Medad are prophesying in the camp. His lieutenant, Joshua, says, "My lord Moses, forbid them." But Moses replies, "Are you envious for my sake? Would to God that *all* the Lord's people were prophets, and that the Lord would put his Spirit upon them!" (Num. 11:28–29).

Laypeople can be fully as prophetic as their clergy—sometimes far more so. In our Unitarian Universalist history, for example, many "people in the pews" have been so far-sighted, courageous, and indeed prophetic that they have played unique roles in the shaping of more just and democratic public institutions. We have already mentioned the work of such U.S. Unitarians as Dorothea Dix, on behalf of mental health care; or Horace Mann, on behalf of free universal public education. We could add Susan B. Anthony, a Unitarian layperson from Rochester, New York, who co-led the long campaign for women's suffrage in the United States.

In Canada, her counterpart was a woman named Emily Jennings Stowe—not only a social activist, but also the first officially sanctioned female doctor in her country. With her resolve toughened by the struggle for professional training and recognition, she devoted her life to ensuring that "the University [open] its doors to women, so that they may have the same chance to learn as men." She founded the Women's College Hospital in Toronto in 1883, and her daughter, Augusta Stowe Gullen, was the first woman to graduate from a Canadian medical school. Three-quarters of a century after her death, in 1981 the Canadian government honored Dr. Stowe by issuing a special stamp to commemorate her life and work.

How can an individual or a religious community attempt to live in the spirit of such prophetic women and men? I am convinced that there are at least four ways, and their right relation must be kept in mind. The first is through concrete acts of human service. "I was hungry and you gave me food; I was thirsty and you gave me drink; I was a stranger and you gave me shelter; naked, and you clothed me; I was sick and you visited me; I was in prison and you came unto me" (Matt. 25:35–36). Traditionally, this constitutes the broad base of what I would call the "pyramid of religious response."

The foundation, or base, of this pyramid is hands-on service, programs where we roll up our sleeves and help one neighbor at a time. Such efforts, of course, are sometimes disparaged by activists as not enough, not directed at the root of things, just band-aid solutions. In a way they are right, for we also need to learn about why people are hungry and homeless, or denied health care or human rights.

A second function then, of social responsibility in our churches and fellowships is moral reflection and social education. Unitarian Universalists often sponsor local public forums for the discussion of social issues in a broad religious and ethical context. At their best, these occasions promote deeper moral dialogue and religious understanding.

Third, our religious communities often support and encourage individual members and friends who feel called to "make their witness" on issues of conscience. We may not always agree, or understand, but we do nurture. In one generation it may be the admission of women to medical school, in another, the desegregation of public restaurants, a protest at a nuclear testing site, or a quiet demonstration—I attended one the other day against the efforts of the Rumanian government to uproot and destroy the villages and culture of their Hungarian-speaking minorities, including the descendents of Francis David. Our provocation will vary, but we must continually confront the "powers and structures of evil."

Finally, there are occasions when corporate, as well as individual, religious social action is appropriate. In Poland, I saw a play with a human rights theme. When banned by the censors from the public theater, it reopened in the courtyard of a local church. In the same spirit, many of our congregations provide sanctuary for refugees from political violence in Central America. Far more substantive than mere resolutions, such forms of concrete corporate action are not to be entered into lightly or unadvisedly. They constitute the highest and riskiest part of my pyramid of response.

It is often tempting to begin the other way—to try to make the pyramid stand on the verbal or symbolic point of some corporate resolutions or seemingly dramatic (though often risk-free) symbolic action. The temptations here are subtle, but insidious.

First, there is the temptation to become known, inexpensively, as prophetic or courageous. Often this means doing or saying something that has no real moral authority. Such authority can only be won through concrete acts of service and through the tough work of building a moral consensus through study, dialogue, and support for diverse witness. Although it is tempting to try to make a big "splash," I believe it is better to rely on what William James called "those tiny invisible molecular moral forces that work from individual to individual, creeping through the crannies of the world like so many rootlets, or like the capillary action of oozing water, yet which, if you give them time, will rend the hardest monuments of human pride."

Second, there is the temptation to what I call "vicarious atonement"—that is, the desire for someone else to perform the sacrifices needed to atone for the sins of the world. This is one doctrine we religious liberals supposedly do not believe. But this is the problem when we merely proclaim to the universe in general our suggestions about how things might better be done.

The covenantal spirit of love in diversity may result in joint witness and action. But that spirit is more likely to be kept whole, without needless divisiveness, if we keep the pyramid broadly based in service, education, dialogue, and nurturance for individual efforts. As James Luther Adams said, it ill-behooves religious liberals to believe in "the immaculate conception of virtue," as though merely holding high ideals or thinking noble thoughts could make us all good. Rather we must strive to practice "the social incarnation of the good we love."

In this regard, I have learned much from the congregations I have served. The people who have inspired me most have been ordinary people, lay people, most

of them unknown, whose words and deeds have testified to the power we have to touch and change the
world. I came of age inspired by public figures such
as John F. Kennedy, who called on us to ask not what
our country could do for us, but what we could do for
our country. But twenty years after his assassination I
was equally inspired by a woman in Dallas, then dying
of cancer, who had been head nurse in the emergency
room to which Kennedy was taken that bleak Novem-
ber day, and who had given all those years and more
to the training of countless emergency medical people.
I was deeply moved by the oratory of Martin Luther
King, Jr., who testified nobly for the dream of a land
in which children would be judged, not by the color
of their skin, but by the content of their character.
But I learned just as much about character from a man
in Tennessee, a white man born in central Mississippi,
who sat in at lunch counters "for the sake of all our
children." And as much as I respect great women of
prophetic vision, such as Susan B. Anthony and the
suffragettes, I equally respect the unheralded, forgotten
women who have served the same vision of equality,
liberty, and human kinship through innumerable
deeds, both great and small.

One symbol of the potential priesthood and prophethood of all believers is a very simple ceremony held
each spring in many of our congregations, the flower
communion. It comes to us from what was, before

World War II, the largest Unitarian congregation in the world, in Prague, Czechoslovakia. In the 1920s the minister there, Norbert Capek, designed this communion to include everyone in the congregation, regardless of belief or background—Protestant, Catholic, Jew, or agnostic. Each worshiper is invited to bring a flower or bit of greenery to church, or provided with one on arrival. Each contribution, like the participants, is quite unique. In the course of the service the flowers are collected in baskets, blessed with a prayer written by Capek, and then redistributed. Everyone leaves with a bit of beauty brought by someone else. Capek publicly opposed the Nazis, and died at Dachau. His congregation today is a struggling remnant. The flower communion remains. It reminds us of the perishable gifts each of us can bring to encourage, include, and inspire one another. It perpetuates his memory, and that of other martyrs, and helps renew our awareness of "all those known and unknown, remembered and forgotten" who even now live as true servants of humankind.

Prague gave us another symbol of our faith: the flaming chalice. In the 1400s a preacher in that city, Jan Hus, anticipated later reforms by conducting worship, not in Latin, but in language the people could comprehend. He also gave them not only the bread at communion, but the wine, the chalice then reserved for the clergy. In 1415, at the Council of Constance, Hus met his predictable fate: condemned for heresy, he too was burned at the stake. But the flame of his death was linked by his followers to the chalice of salvation which he had offered to all people.

In 1939 a Czech artist named Hans Deutsch was asked to design a symbol for the Unitarian Service Committee, which had been formed to assist people like him to flee from the Nazis. The motif he selected was the flaming chalice. In a simple, stylized modern form, it is used still by the Service Committee. The Unitarian Universalist Association in the meantime has adopted a version which sets the chalice within an overlapping double circle. The chalice is cruciform, but set off center within the circles, just as the Universalists once represented their Christian heritage as but one part of a larger, more universal whole. Its light evokes the eternal flame in the ancient temple at Jerusalem, as well as the lamp of reason, and the flames on the many altars of faith—all very real sources of our living tradition.

The flaming chalice is also more than a symbol. Through the Unitarian Universalist Service Committee, projects of rescue are still undertaken all over the world. As an independent, nonsectarian expression of our Unitarian Universalist traditions of humanitarian and prophetic concern, the Service Committee cooperates with many international relief efforts in crises where human lives are at stake. But it also does much more—many things that go largely unheralded even in our own circles. Far from doing missionary work or proselytizing, the UUSC has shown leadership in working to empower people to resist and change oppressive conditions, to educate and mobilize groups for service and action. Its model-setting development projects work with local partners promoting human freedom and self-determination in Africa, India, Central America, and the Caribbean. Here at home, it speaks on behalf of those threatened with violence through misguided applications of U.S. foreign policy, and it carries out a domestic program aimed at children in poverty, children at risk.

The number of Unitarian Universalists in the world is not impressive: 200,000 in North America; 80,000 in Rumania and Hungary; perhaps 10,000 more in Great Britain and scattered elsewhere in Europe; small indigenous groups in India, the Philippines, and Nigeria. But like Quakers, we have an influence that far exceeds our small numbers. Other groups have far more followers, but we seem to produce some remarkably prophetic social leaders. Remembered and forgotten, martyred and living, such prophets attempt to act according to their faith, not their fear; to answer fear with love; to nurture human hope; and to serve the prophethood of all believers.

One Unitarian Universalist layperson, Ed Schempp, from Barrington, New Jersey, has summarized our faith quite simply:

> Unitarian Universalism is a fierce belief in the way of freedom and reverence for the sacred dignity of each individual. With Jefferson, we have sworn eternal hostility against every tyranny over the mind.
>
> Unitarian Universalism is cooperation with a universe that created us; it is celebration of life; it is being in love with goodness and justice; it is a sense of humor about absolutes.
>
> Unitarian Universalism is faith in people, hope for tomorrow's child, confidence in a continuity that spans all time. It looks not to a perfect heaven, but toward a good earth. It is respectful of the past, but not limited to it. It is trust in growing and conspiracy with change. It is spiritual responsibility for a moral tomorrow.

PART 3

Wisdom from the world's religions which inspires us in our ethical and spiritual life.

5

The Cathedral of the World

Forrest Church

I think that one of our most important tasks is to convince others that there's nothing to fear in difference; that difference, in fact, is one of the healthiest and most invigorating of human characteristics without which life would become meaningless. Here lies the power of the liberal way: not in making the whole world Unitarian, but in helping ourselves and others to see some of the possibilities inherent in viewpoints other than one's own; in encouraging the free interchange of ideas; in welcoming fresh approaches to the problems of life; in urging the fullest, most vigorous use of critical self-examination.

—*Adlai Stevenson, Unitarian layperson*

When you and I look at these trees, these flowers, anything at all, we are the universe looking at its handiwork. You have perhaps seen the pattern of cross and yarn called the "eye of God" made first in our Southwest in homage to the sun. We, too, all of us together, all the eyes of all the creatures, are the eye of God. That is why we need each other,

our many ways of seeing, that together we may rejoice, and
see clearly, and find the many keys to abundant life.

—*Greta W. Crosby, Unitarian Universalist minister*

IMAGINE AWAKING one morning from a deep and
dreamless sleep to find yourself in the nave of a vast
cathedral. Like a child newborn, untutored save to
moisture, nurture, rhythm, and the profound comforts
at the heart of darkness, you open your eyes upon a
world unseen, indeed unimaginable, before. It is a
world of light and dancing shadow, stone and glass,
life and death. This second birth, at once miraculous
and natural, is in some ways not unlike the first. A
new awakening, it consecrates your life with sacraments of pain you do not understand and promised joy
you will never fully call your own.

Such awakenings may happen only once in a lifetime, or many times. But when they do, what you
took for granted before is presented as a gift: difficult,
yet precious and good. Not that you know what to do
with your gift, or even what it really means, only how
much it matters. Awakening to the call stirring deep
within you, the call of life itself—the call of God—
you begin your pilgrimage.

Before you do, look about you; contemplate the
mystery and contemplate with awe. This cathedral is
as ancient as humankind, its cornerstone the first altar,
marked with the tincture of blood and stained with

tears. Search for a lifetime, which is all you are surely given, and you shall never know its limits, visit all its apses, worship at its myriad shrines, nor span its celestial ceiling with your gaze. The builders have worked from time immemorial, destroying and creating, confounding and perfecting, tearing down and raising up arches in this cathedral, butresses and chapels, organs and theaters, chancels and transepts, gargoyles, idols, and icons. Not a moment passes without work being begun that shall not be finished in the lifetime of the architects who planned it, the patrons who paid for it, the builders who construct it, or the expectant worshipers. And not a moment passes without the dreams of long-dead dreamers being outstripped, shattered, or abandoned, giving way to new visions, each immortal in reach, ephemeral in grasp.

Welcome to the cathedral of the world.

Above all else, contemplate the windows. In the cathedral of the world there are windows without number, some long forgotten, covered with many patinas of dust, others revered by millions, the most sacred of shrines. Each in its own way is beautiful. Some are abstract, others representational; some dark and meditative, others bright and dazzling. Each tells a story about the creation of the world, the meaning of history, the purpose of life, the nature of humankind, the mystery of death. The windows of the cathedral are where the light shines in.

As with all extended metaphors, this one is imperfect. The light of God ("God" is not God's name, but our name for that which is greater than all and yet present in each) not only shines down upon us, but also out from within us. Together with the windows, the darkness and the light, we are part of the cathedral, not apart from it. Together we comprise an interdependent web of being; if the cathedral is built out of star stuff, so are we. But we are that part (that known part) that contemplates the meaning of the whole. Because the cathedral is so vast, our time so short, and our vision so dim, we are able to contemplate only a tiny part of the cathedral, explore a few apses, reflect upon the play of darkness and light through a few of its windows. Yet, since the whole—holographically or organically—is contained in each of the parts, as we ponder and act upon the insight from our ruminations, we may discover meanings that give coherence and meaning both to it and to us.

This is Universalism.

Fundamentalists of the right and left claim that the light shines through their window only. Skeptics can make a similar mistake, only to draw the opposite conclusion. Seeing the bewildering variety of windows and observing the folly of the worshipers, they conclude that there is no light. But the windows are not the light. The whole light—God, Truth, call it what you will—is beyond our perceiving. God is veiled. Some people have trouble believing in a God who looks into any eyes but theirs. Others have trouble believing in a God they cannot see. But the fact that none of us can look directly into God's eyes certainly does not mean that in the light and the darkness, mysterious and unknowable, God is not there.

Religion is dangerous, of course, because its power is independent of the universal validity of its claims. Every generation has its terrorists for Truth and God, hard-bitten zealots for whom the world is large enough for only one true faith. They have been taught to worship at one window, and then to prove their faith by throwing rocks through other peoples' windows. Tightly drawn, their logic makes a demonic kind of sense: (1) religious answers respond to life and death questions, which happen to be the most important questions of all; (2) you and I may come up with different answers; (3) if you are right, I must be wrong; (4) but I can't be wrong, because my salvation hinges upon being right; therefore (5), short of abandoning my own faith and embracing yours, in order to secure my salvation I am driven to ignore, convert, or destroy you.

One impartial response to this war of conflicting convictions is to reject religion, to distance ourselves from those who attempt, always imperfectly, to interpret the cosmic runes and gauge their responses accordingly. There are two problems with this approach. One is that such rejection deprives us of a potentially deep encounter with the mysterious forces that impel our being and the opportunity to illuminate, if but partially, its meaning. The second is that none of us is able to resist interpreting the cosmic runes. Consequently, not only the world's religions, but every ideology, every scientific worldview, every aesthetic school, has its windows in the cathedral of the world. In each the light and darkness mingle in ways that suggest meaning for those whose angle of vision is tilted in that particular direction. Attracted to the patterns of refracted light, the playing of shadows, the partial clarification of reality, these people are also worshipers; their windows too become shrines.

None of us is fully able to perceive the truth that shines through another person's window, nor the falsehood that we may perceive as truth. Thus, we can easily mistake another's good for evil, and our own evil for good. A true, and therefore humble, universalist theology addresses this tendency, which we all share, while speaking eloquently to the overarching crisis of our times: dogmatic division in an ever more intimate, fractious, and yet interdependent world. It posits the following fundamental principles:

1. There is one Reality, one Truth, one God.
2. This Reality shines through every window in the cathedral (and out from every eye).

3. No one can perceive it directly, the mystery being forever veiled.

4. Yet, on the cathedral floor and in the eyes of each beholder, refracted and reflected through different windows in different ways, it plays in patterns that suggest meaning, challenging us to interpret and live by the meaning as best we can.

5. Therefore, each window illumines Truth (with a large T) in a different way, leading to different truths (with a small t), and these in differing measure according to the insight and receptivity of the beholder.

Among other things, this theology suggests that we must acknowledge the partial nature of our understanding; respect insights that differ from our own; and not only defend the rights of others to believe their own truths so long as they do not deny us the same privilege, but also credit them with a measure of truth (with a small *t*) even though it may conflict with the truth that we embrace.

Even universalism can be perverted. One way is to elevate one truth into a universal truth: "My church is the one true church." This might be called imperialistic universalism. Another, leading to reductionistic universalism, is to reduce distinctive truths to a lowest common denominator: "All religion is merely a set of variations upon the golden rule." The universalism I aspire to does neither. It holds that the same light shines through all our windows, but that each window is different. The windows modify the light, refracting it in myriad ways, shaping it in different patterns, suggesting different meanings.

This is not a simple appeal for relativism (reductionistic universalism). For each of us to grow in faith and understanding, we can do no better than to cultivate and develop the particular meanings reflected in our own traditions and cultures. Aspiring to see the refracted light as clearly as we can, we act upon our insights as best we may. I'm suggesting a new theological model, in which one light (Unitarianism) shines through many windows (Universalism) in various, yet telling ways.

With my cathedral metaphor, I introduce the third source of our common faith: wisdom from the world's religions which inspires us in our ethical and spiritual life. So long as we avoid the smorgasbord approach to religion (reductionistic universalism: a little too much of everything, leaving us with a stomach ache and a confused palate), we assume an almost unique position among the world's faiths. We draw inspiration from other religions as well as our own. Within our churches we acknowledge the presence of many different windows, celebrate a wide variety of festivals in an attempt to divine the essential meaning of each, and—at our best—truly welcome and respect the insights of others.

We are always seeking new guidance from ancient sources for the shaping of our ethical and spiritual lives. This has its dangers, for we may trivialize the faith of another by trying to appropriate its essence. But as long as we remember this, by remaining open to the insights of others we may augment our own cherished traditions and expand the scope of our faith.

A Unitarian minister, James Freeman Clarke, first introduced the study of world religions as a fertile field for intellectual and spiritual growth. Together with Ralph Waldo Emerson and Margaret Fuller, Clarke was a charter member of the Transcendental Club, and his interest in world religions initially was inspired by transcendentalist reflections upon the "oversoul," that which is greater than all and yet present in each, both overarching and inspiring every individual and every faith. He was minister for seven years in Louisville; editor of *The Messenger,* a short-lived but vital magazine, in which works by Unitarians such as Emerson, Oliver Wendell Holmes, and Orestes Bronson were published; he was Secretary of the American Unitarian Association; professor of Natural Religion and Christian Doctrine at Harvard; a political activist, in large part responsible for securing the presidential nomination for Grover Cleveland in 1884; and, for forty-three years, he served as minister of the Church of the Disciples in Boston, which he founded in 1841. Clarke was one of the most influential Unitarians of his day.

He also wrote more than thirty books, including his ground-breaking two-volume study, *Ten Great Religions,* the first of its kind to be published in America. Though his thesis was patronizing (namely, that each of these religions represented a way station on the road to Christianity), these volumes raised the veil from religions that before had only been known in parody and caricature.

Just before the turn of the century another Unitarian minister, Jenkin Lloyd Jones, a founder of and evangelist for the Western Unitarian Conference, broke important new ground by organizing the Parliament of Religions, which met at the 1893 Chicago Columbian Exposition. Representatives from many of the great faiths came together there for the first time, giving all the participants, many of whom were Unitarians and Universalists, a first-hand introduction to each of their respective views. Jones himself envisioned this conclave as the first step toward a universal religion that would unite all believers, a modern religion, illustrated by all scriptures yet transcending the particularities of each. He, and many Unitarians and Universalists to follow, believed that once simplified to their essence all religions were one. This corrected Clarke's Christian bias, only to replace it with an idealistic and superficial glossing of the profound and unique characteristics at the heart of each of the world's religions. Nonetheless, following the transcendentalists' philosophical lead, Clarke and Jones helped to expand Unitarianism beyond a liberal Christian faith to a faith that might best be described not as non-Christian, but as more than Christian.

Today, this expansiveness is most evident in two places: Unitarian Universalist worship and religious education. In worship the shift is marked most dramatically by the publication in 1964 of *Hymns for the Celebration of Life,* its key editor being the Universalist minister Kenneth Patton. A distinguished poet in his own right, Patton has devoted his life to the writing of hymns and verse and the gathering of worship materials from all the world's religions as well as from secular poets, philosophers, and public servants. When serving as minister of the Charles Street Meeting House in Boston, he established a humanistic chapel of all faiths, which were emblematically represented by symbols of the world's religions in a mural of the cosmos covering one entire wall. The worship materials themselves—not only new texts for hymns but also hundreds of responsive and unison readings—were collected and written by Patton over the years, and published by his own press in a series of anthologies. As a member of the commission that produced *Hymns for the Celebration of Life* ("the blue hymnal"—soon to be supplanted by a gender-inclusive, and even more wide-ranging update), he collected many of the hymns and readings, interspersed them with more traditional materials, and thereby brought Unitarian Universalist worship more fully in line with what had by the mid-twentieth century become mainstream Unitarian and Universalist theology. Patton and his co-commissioners were acting in the spirit of Thomas Jefferson, who said, "Were I to be the founder of a new sect, I would call them Apiarians, and, after the example of the bee, advise them to extract the honey of every sect."

In religious education, the shift from Christian education to something far more encompassing was sponsored by a woman who came to Unitarianism late in life, the great religious educator Sophia Lyon Fahs. Director of the church school at New York's Riverside Church during the years Harry Emerson Fosdick served as minister, and instructor in Christian education at Union Theological Seminary, Fahs had already sought to transform religious education in the mainstream liberal Protestant denominations when in 1937, at the age of sixty-one, she was called by the American Unitarian Association president, Frederick May Eliot, to revise and expand the existing Unitarian religious education curricula. First in the New Beacon Series, and then in several other books, most importantly, *Today's Children and Yesterday's Heritage* and her anthology of stories, *From Long Ago and Many Lands,* Fahs revolutionized religious education. Abandoning the rote recitation (and coloring!) of Bible stories, she crafted curricula designed to draw from the child's own experiences, while employing stories from all religious and cultural traditions. Sophia Lyon Fahs entered the Unitarian ministry in 1959 at Cedar Lane Church in Bethesda, Maryland, at the age of eighty-two. She even preached her own ordination sermon, and no one doubted she had chosen the best person for the job.

Fahs was fond of quoting another great liberal religious educator and contemporary, Angus MacLean, who said that we are not merely the "bellhops of history passing the baggage of one generation on to another." We have to unpack that baggage and make it our own. "Culture makes it possible for human relations to bridge the grave, for individuals who are so short of days to live with a wisdom derived from the dawn of time," he went on to say. "Our job is not to worship history and culture like fetishes, but to feed them into our living, creative stream of personal life for spiritual and intellectual reprocessing."

In worship, when a reading, or hymn, or story from one of the world's great religions strikes a responsive chord in our heart, it becomes a part of our own growing and changing tradition. We may not understand it as it originally was understood, or interpret it as it originally was interpreted, but the light refracted through other windows when mingled with that which shines through our own can enhance our vision, and expand our faith. Perhaps as important, it can engender humility by reminding us that we have limits and by suggesting the wonderful array of possible interpretations of what it means to be alive and to die.

Some parents do not want to impose religious training upon their children, preferring instead to let them make up their own minds when they come of age. This stance is only superficially "liberal," for it deprives the children of any criteria for judging. The distinctive feature of Unitarian Universalist education is that young people are introduced to many religious traditions, challenged to formulate their own beliefs, and encouraged to respect the beliefs of others. As a Unitarian Universalist religious educator, Jean Starr Williams writes, "We think of each person and each constellation of persons in our community as being in need of intellectual enlightenment. It is not enough to know only the worlds we ourselves move in. Each of us must be invited, encouraged, even prodded to look beyond our immediate surroundings to the wider world around us. We need to strive toward an educated outlook, which has as its roots a longing for justice, compassion, and peace for all humankind."

In *From Long Ago and Many Lands,* Sophia Lyon Fahs tells a Buddhist story from India, of which my "Cathedral of the World" is a variation or reprise. A group of seekers were devoting their life to reflection upon the great religious questions, such as "Does a person live again after he or she dies?" or "What is God like?" Since each of them had come up with different answers, they often got into furious arguments. "I'm right and you're wrong," one would say. "No, you're wrong and I'm right," another would reply. To resolve these disputes, they presented their beliefs to the great teacher, Buddha, who would tell them who was right and who was wrong. He answered by telling them this story.

Once upon a time there was a king who asked his servant to bring to him all the people in the town who were born blind, and also an elephant. "This is an elephant," he said to them. "Each one of you may touch this elephant, and when you have done so I want you to tell me what an elephant is like." He let one touch the elephant's head, another its ears, and others its tusks, trunk, legs, back, and tail.

"Your Majesty, an elephant is like a large waterpot," said the one who had only touched the elephant's head. "Your Majesty, he is wrong," rejoined the one who had touched the ears. "An elephant is like a flat basket." The others insisted as adamantly upon the insights drawn from their own limited experience, respectively comparing the elephant to the sharp end of a plow, a thin rope, a big crib full of wheat, four pillars and, finally, a fan.

Upon finishing this parable, Buddha said to the seekers who had been quarreling over the nature of God and the afterlife, "How can you be so sure of what you cannot see? We all are like unsighted people in this world. We cannot see God. Nor can we know what is going to happen after we die. Each one of you may be partly right in your answers. Yet none of you is fully right. Let us not quarrel over what we cannot be sure of."

One Truth, many truths; one God, many faiths; one light (Unitarianism), many windows (Universalism). This is why we number as one of the sources for the living tradition we share "wisdom from the world's religions which inspires us in our ethical and spiritual life." Among other things, it reminds us to be humble, especially when we are sure we are right.

6

Dialogue

John A. Buehrens

A dialogue by members of the world community which promotes peace requires risk. The risk includes the possibility
of arousing anger and hostility in the expression of strongly
held conflicting views. Perhaps an even greater risk is the
surprise in receiving new insights that require changing
your own perspective. It is possible that you could discover
unexplored horizons of meaning and truth. In real engage-
ment with another person, you cannot fully foresee what
will happen. At the same time, risk must be matched by
trust. To expose yourself to the analysis and challenge of another person requires trust. Dialogue depends on trust that
the other person is also caring, is secure enough in his or
her view to allow for differences, and is open to learning
new dimensions of his or her orientation that may be evoked
in dialogue.

> —*Frederick J. Streng, professor of world religions
> and Unitarian Universalist layperson*

It matters what we believe. Some beliefs are like walled gar-
dens. They encourage exclusiveness and the feeling of being

especially privileged. Other beliefs are expansive and lead the way into wider and deeper sympathies.

—Sophia Lyon Fahs, Unitarian Universalist minister
and religious educator

I HAVE ONE PROBLEM with the image of the "cathedral of the world." Within the cathedral, no one seems to be talking to anyone else.

"Walk together, talk together, O ye peoples of the earth. Then and only then shall ye have peace." This admonition by a Hindu sage serves as the motto for AFS International Scholarships, a program founded after World War II by members of the corps of volunteer ambulance drivers, the American Field Service. When I was sixteen, I was lucky enough to be chosen to study abroad for a year under one of their programs. I spent the year in Italy, living with a family in Milan and going to a large Jesuit high school. Four years later I returned to Italy for a convocation of exchange students from all over the world.

Last year my daughter Mary had a similar experience. She and three other eleven-year-olds from Manhattan represented the United States at a Children's International Summer Village. This program takes children old enough to be away from home for a month, but before they are as self-conscious as adolescents often are. At this age they meet others more easily. Twelve delegations, each made up of two boys, two girls, and a teacher, form a village. Mary's experience, like mine, was in northern Italy and has created a nice bond between us. The children she met in the village were from Thailand, Japan, the Soviet Union, Argentina, Norway, Rumania, Britain, Brazil, Turkey, Spain, and Italy, plus staff from Lebanon and the Ivory Coast. After a month she came back having matured a year and having made friends from a dozen different cultures and faiths.

While my daughter was in Italy I was at Stanford, attending the Triennial Congress of the International Association for Religious Freedom. This is the interfaith international body of religious liberals to which our Unitarian Universalist Association in North America belongs. At this gathering, our religious commitment to a dynamic pluralism came alive for me in new ways: being instructed in the Japanese tea ceremony by members of the lay Buddhist organization, the Rissho Kosei Kai; conversations with a young theologian from the Unitarian seminary in Cluj, Rumania; a dignified woman from the Brahmo Samaj movement of Calcutta, describing efforts in India to empower poor women; a man from Scotland, wearing a kilt, explaining the reverence for nature behind the rites performed by a Shinto priest; and a group of young adults from the Philippines, describing their volunteer work in teaching rural children to read. In conjunction with the Congress, an important meeting on Buddhist-Christian dialogue also took place.

"Dialogue," said one participant, "has a new connotation in contemporary religious discourse. Here attitudes of cultural and religious superiority are yielding to those of humility, when people of different faiths share with one another what they have inherited from the past as well as their personal understanding and experience of that faith. This involves no compromise in integrity. Instead, it results in personal enrichment between people of different traditions."

Mircea Eliade, the late professor of world religions at the University of Chicago, used to talk about the spiritual search of many young Americans who would come to his classes on the Eastern traditions. Some actually took up a demanding discipline like Zen meditation; most did not. But he found that a more profound understanding of human spirituality would often lead them into a new, transformed relationship with the Western religious tradition from which they had been estranged.

Eliade used a story from the Hasidic Jews of Eastern Europe to illustrate his observation. Once upon a time in Krakow, a rabbi dreamt three times that an angel told him to go to Livovna, and that in front of the palace there, near a bridge, he would find a treasure. When the rabbi arrived in Livovna, he told his story to a sentinel who told him that he, too, had had a dream in which he was told to go to a rabbi's house in Krakow, where a treasure was buried in front of the fireplace. So the rabbi went home and dug at his own hearthstone and found a treasure.

"This means," Eliade would explain, "that the spiritual treasure is already there, with you, in the heart. But often you have to go somewhere else, to another teacher outside your tradition, to find the treasure. To find yourself, you sometimes must go to a stranger."

The secret to dialogue is passing over and then returning. We pass over into an appreciative attempt to understand the experience and insight of another person or tradition. When we return to ourselves, as we inevitably do in one way or another, we are no longer precisely the same person we were before. We are changed by the experience, in some way transformed and enlarged. This pattern may be a paradigm for spiritual growth in our pluralistic world. Encounters with people of different backgrounds, cultures, and religious outlooks are becoming more and more frequent as population grows and our world shrinks. In such encounters there is sure to be some conflict. Differences can be threatening. Traditional Iranian Muslim leaders can feel threatened by Western cultural imperialism. A secular American parent can feel threatened by a young adult child's devotion to some Eastern form of spirituality. But when the spirit of passing over and returning prevails, dialogue, mutual respect, and enrichment are made possible. Differences are not abolished, nor is personal identity, but people are transformed in the direction of a larger wholeness.

One of the religious geniuses of our century, Mahatma Gandhi, embodied the passing over and returning paradigm. Raised a devout Hindu, by a progressive father and a traditionalist mother, in a sect influenced by monotheistic Islam, he traveled to Britain as a young man to become a barrister. There, while eating in vegetarian restaurants to uphold his Hindu precepts, he came into contact with Westerners interested in Eastern religion. Through them, he was introduced to new books—to theosophy, to Tolstoy's idealism, to Thoreau's transcendentalism and civil disobedience, and to the Gospel stories about Jesus.

But Gandhi did not just treat the new ideas as bookish theory. As a young lawyer among the Indians of South Africa dealing with racial discrimination, he began to experiment with applying the ideals of Western spirituality in his dealings with self-professed Christians—even when they abused him. By mid-life he was back in India, living out a new and transformed understanding of his own Hindu faith and morality, one both more authentically inward and deeply influenced by his encounters with Christianity. Rejecting discrimination against Hindus without caste, Gandhi called them not "untouchables," but *harijans,* or "children of God,"—much as Jesus might have. He gave a new interpretation to the *Bhagavad Gita* and its concept of *dharma,* or duty. Conflict may be inevitable, as Krishna tells the warrior Arjuna in that Hindu classic. But for Gandhi, Arjuna's duty (and ours) is not fighting in the traditional, unproductive way; it is the use of *satyagraha,* or "truth force," which in practical terms means fighting prejudice and injustice with nonviolent resistance.

Looking at the religious aspects of many intergroup conflicts, at the violence carried out by zealots in the name of religion, some people conclude that the world would be safer "religion-free." They may even try living that way themselves. But too often they only practice a form of self-delusion. Nature abhors a vacuum and so does the human spirit. As C. S. Lewis said, the opposite of a belief in God is not a belief in nothing; it is a belief in anything. Sweep the demon of religion out the door and, like the story in the Gospels, you may only succeed in making room for an evil spirit worse than the first—this one accompanied by seven friends (Luke 11:24–26; Matt. 12:43–45). Zealous atheism can perform this role of demonic pseudoreligion. At the group and ideological level, so can many other *isms,* such as tribalism, nationalism, materialism, and scientism. At the personal level, individuals can trade an authentic faith for such pseudofaiths (and demons) as careerism, hedonism, and alcoholism. Over the years I have become convinced, as Jung was, that the problems in the world are not caused by faith; they are caused by the lack of authenticity and openness in faith, and by the pseudofaiths that substitute for a healthy spirituality of mutual respect and dialogue.

Beyond this, our growing awareness of the world as a global village requires that we seek to understand, and wherever possible, respect our neighbors' views. In each of the world's great faiths there is something authentic to appreciate and to hear. As my friend Jacob Trapp writes:

Each of the great religions has a distinctive note,
to be likened to the strings of a harp.

In Hinduism it is the note of spirit:
a universe throbbing with divine energy and meaning.

In Buddhism it is the wisdom of self-discipline:
quenching the fire of desire in the cool waters of
meditation.

In Confucianism it is reciprocity:
mutual consideration is the basis of society.

In Taoism it is to conquer by inaction:
be lowly and serviceable, like a brook;
become rich by sharing.

In Judaism it is exodus from bondage:
the covenant of responsibility in freedom.

In Islam it is the note of submission:
"Our God and your God is one, to whom we are
self-surrendered."

In Christianity it is that all may become one:
"This is my body broken for you."
"Inasmuch as you have done it to one of the least
of these."

The issues of interfaith dialogue and mutual respect
are not only global or theoretical. In our shrinking
world, in which cultures and religions are increasingly
more likely to confront one another, they come down
to a very personal and practical level when people from
different religious backgrounds meet one another, fall
in love, and decide to marry. Here, like most Unitarian
Universalist ministers, I have a good deal of direct
experience.

Not long ago I met with a New York couple in
their late twenties who asked me to preside at their
wedding. The bride-to-be was from Punjab, in Northern India. Her groom was also from South Asia, but
from the island country of Sri Lanka. There the religious majority is Buddhist, but the groom was raised
a Methodist. The bride's family is Hindu. Both have
parents who now live in the United States and are

citizens here. I delicately inquired whether either family had raised objections to the marriage on religious grounds.

"Oh, yes," she said, "but they all seem more relieved that we're finally getting married. By their standards, you see, we're both rather *old* not to be married already and parents of a family."

"Have they asked how you will raise the children?"

"Yes," he replied, "they have asked about this."

"We will raise the children as Christians," she chimed in. For a moment I was unsure: Was she saying this thinking it would somehow please me? to convince me to do the wedding?

"But not fundamentalists," he added quickly.

"We live in this country now," she explained.

"We'll look for a church that will respect us both," he added hopefully.

I encouraged them in their search, and mentioned a Unitarian Universalist congregation in the community where they had bought a house. "You'll find that members of our congregations tend to come from a fairly wide variety of backgrounds and beliefs. We respect diversity and affirm an underlying spiritual unity. You may want to visit, or to learn more about how we conduct religious education for our children. But you don't need to make any commitments to *me* if I'm to perform your wedding—only to one another. I suggest we concentrate on planning a ceremony that's both inclusive and honest—one we can all feel comfortable celebrating. Now tell me what ideas and plans you may already have."

No couple contemplating a "mixed marriage" is really like any other. Each is unique. People vary greatly in how much diversity, and of what sort, they can tolerate. Family attitudes also make a big difference. I am particularly sensitive to these things. My wife, Gwen, and I constitute such a mixed marriage—and a professional one at that. Gwen is a priest in the Episcopal church. We met when we were both students in seminary—she at Yale and I at Harvard. We were doing our "clinical pastoral education" together as chaplains-in-training at a hospital in Boston. In 1972, three days after we were married, Gwen was ordained as one of the first women deacons in her church. I was ordained a year later, and after a long struggle, she too entered the full-time parish ministry, as the first woman in the Dallas diocese to become a priest.

"Remember which vows came first," her first bishop told us when we married. Believe me, we have tried. Today we feel very fortunate. Gwen serves a parish just nine blocks from All Souls. We live in housing on the grounds there. So I am the Unitarian minister who lives at the Church of the Holy Trinity! The irony delights us. We understand when people are baffled; when they shake their heads and say, "My, my, you two must have some *interesting* discussions." The truth is that most of our debates are rather more mundane: about the unholy trinity of checkbook, chores, and children, not the holy one. We do our best to support each other's efforts at ministry.

Our daughters, Erica and Mary, have been thoroughly exposed to both traditions. At a certain point they were told, "This year you can go to either Sunday school. You choose, but you can't stay home." I might have guessed how things would turn out. When Erica was two and a half, we found her one day with a towel draped down her back like a vestment, holding a hymnal (upside down), and marching around the couch singing "The Hokie Pokie." Obviously, an Episcopalian! This year she played a part in the Holy Trinity youth group's production of *Godspell*. In June she was confirmed by the bishop, with Dad in attendance and Mom assisting. Mary, on the other hand, goes to All Souls. She loved her Sunday school class this year, which studied stories from Genesis and Exodus—putting Jacob and Rachel on trial in the matter of Esau's birthright, and conducting a protest march against Moses and Aaron, with signs reading "Meat, not Manna!" "Impeach Moses!" and "Back to Egypt." When she grows up, Mary says, she might like to be Jewish.

Who knows? After all, in our society, more and more people make their decisions about religious identity as young adults. Gwen and I both did. Gwen was raised a Methodist; I, a nominal Roman Catholic. Both of us had parents with different religious backgrounds. We made our own decisions about where we belonged in the religious world before we ever met each other, and we have never tried to convert the other. (Well, *almost* never.) For the most part our differences are not threatening; they enrich and deepen our own understandings of religious living.

But we know other couples for whom having a religious community in common, for themselves and their children, is important—as it obviously is for the couple I recently married. We Unitarian Universalists have both. There are couples who have chosen us because one was of one tradition, one of another. For them Unitarian Universalism held the promise of an affirming common ground. We have other members whose spouses are not Unitarian Universalists, but active in another church or synagogue. Still others retain some previous ties of their own. As I sometimes tell people, tongue in cheek, "We're the one church to have, if you're having more than one!" I say this because we affirm diversity, dialogue, and personal choice in religious living, and tend not to be possessive, or easily threatened by other involvements.

Today the term "mixed marriage" is taking on an ever-broader meaning in the religious context, but in our society it traditionally has suggested Protestant-Catholic or, especially, Christian-Jewish unions. In their book *Mixed Blessings,* Paul and Rachel Cowan write about the latter, and warn their readers against dismissing too lightly the issues of religion and spirituality. There are some "hidden time bombs" in such an approach, they say. One is children. Another has to do with death—both our own and the death of people we love. Paul Cowan was a Jew who had little religious identification with Judaism—until his father died, that is, and until he visited Jerusalem. Rachel Cowan was raised a Unitarian. Now she has converted, Paul has died, and Rachel will soon be ordained a rabbi.

Conversion is one answer to differences in religious background. Two affiliations is another. The common ground of a Unitarian Universalist congregation represents a third. This may begin as a compromise, but the solution works best when it does not end there. In our congregations, rather than avoid differences in background and spirituality, each partner can encourage the other in an ever-deeper process of spiritual growth. Inevitably the process includes exploring and affirming one's own roots. When that is not done, I agree with the Cowans: there *are* hidden time bombs.

One cost of avoiding religion altogether may be spiritual isolation. Too often today couples are already socially isolated. Their friends are colleagues at work. They live away from their families. Aside from parents, or perhaps a boss, they have few models for the next stage of life. If nothing else, a religious community, like a recovery of roots, can provide one with a spiritual extended family, and a safe context for discussing the deeper issues arising from success or failure, grief or illness, or the ultimate questions of good and evil. Having raised their children in a spiritual vacuum, apart from any religious discussion or community, committed secularists are sometimes shocked when their offspring suddenly join a high-demand cult or follow a seductive guru. Nature abhors a vacuum, and so does the human spirit. The lure of the various *isms,* though hardly unknown to religious people, may be even more intense for those who avoid religion.

As with most Unitarian Universalist ministers, when I meet with Christian-Jewish engaged couples, I am careful not to decide in advance where they belong, to proselytize, or to dissuade. I begin by exploring their attitudes and family backgrounds. Sometimes I conclude, "I think you should be married by a rabbi." Or by a priest and a rabbi. Or by a justice of the peace. Or I may recommend some counseling first. Often I make referrals to couples' therapists, to receptive rabbis or priests, or to support groups for similar couples. I also explain the rather diverse ideas our culture has of what is happening in the marriage ceremony.

One is the secular-legal interpretation. A license is obtained from the county clerk. The state authorizes clergy to "solemnize marriage" on behalf of their religious communities. Will Campbell, a Southern Baptist preacher who believes, as I do, in both the separation of church and state and in the spiritual character of all true marriage, suggests a procedure I sometimes describe to couples. "I sign the license before the ceremony," says Will. "Then I seal it in the envelope to go back to the courthouse and I throw it in the corner yelling, 'Render unto Caesar the things that are Caesar's!' I then remind the couple that all that piece of paper is good for is, God forbid, to go back to the courthouse—and sue one another for divorce—and that they're about to go out and, in the face of God and everybody, say some things that darn well better mean something, had better evoke the spirit of an enduring love."

Another interpretation puts the focus on communal religious blessings. In a sacramental understanding of marriage, as among Roman Catholics, the key moment of the wedding is not the exchange of vows, but the blessing of the marriage, with the couple kneeling before the priest. The vows can be done elsewhere. But the church's rules are about how and to whom such sacramental blessing can be imparted. Generally speaking, divorced parties need not apply. In Jewish weddings, marriage to a Gentile is problematic because the ceremony represents "the opening of a new household in the community of Israel." That is why it is conducted under a canopy, a *chupah*. Many rabbis refuse to officiate or co-officiate at any mixed marriage, but those who will often want to know, "To what extent will this be a *Jewish* household?"

I am neither priest, nor a rabbi, nor a justice of the peace. When I preside at a marriage, like most Unitarian Universalist ministers, I see myself principally assisting two people affirm their covenantal relationship. Having already agreed privately to love and support each other, they come forward publicly to articulate that commitment, to receive the support and blessings of their families and friends, and to be recognized as a committed couple. "May the blessings that rest on those who truly love rest on you," I often conclude, "and fill you with all love's grace, both now and forever."

But I do not use the same words at all weddings. I am willing to work with couples to shape the ceremony into a personally meaningful and successful celebration. Each of us has his or her own style. For instance, Forrest Church, my colleague in ministry, almost always concludes weddings by saying, "I welcome you to the not always blissful but ever wondrous state of matrimony. I have only this to ask of you. May your hearts be as open as your minds are attentive and discerning. May your lips sing forth the praise of every earthly good. May your souls yearn for truth, to be sought, I believe, in understanding. May your works be of love. May you stand where it shall be right to have stood."

Forrest and I both feel privileged and enriched to serve in a tradition where dynamic religious pluralism and dialogue are fostered. In our congregation we have active groups for Christian Awareness and for Jewish Awareness, a scattering of members from Muslim and Hindu backgrounds, and a number of participants in a Unitarian Universalist Buddhist Fellowship. Our worship is clearly shaped in a pattern that seems Protestant, but really goes back to the early synagogue, with hymns, readings, a sermon, and a benediction. It includes music from the rich heritage of Protestant, Catholic, and Jewish spirituality. Occasionally, we may even use something special, like the Gustav Holst *Hymns from the Rig Veda*. But all variations are developed within the strong, familiar pattern and are consistent with what our worship tradition represents.

If those patterns, like our understandings of marriage, have roots in the Protestant Reformation, it is not simply because that's where our historical roots as a movement lie. It is also where many of us have come from recently. A survey of our backgrounds in the early 1980s showed that 19 percent of all Unitarian Universalists were raised as Methodists—the largest single group among us. A roughly equal number came from other liberal to moderate Protestant denominations, and a slightly smaller number had backgrounds in evangelical or conservative Protestant churches. The number of former Roman Catholics (like myself) seems to be growing, and was very nearly equal to the Methodists. About 5 percent are of Jewish heritage. Some had little or no religious training. Others identify with non-Western religious traditions. Only about 15 percent were born or raised as Unitarian Universalists.

"What?" you may say. "What happens to the children?" Perhaps somewhat surprisingly the truth is that we are not very different from other liberal religious movements. A recent study in the Episcopal church showed that only one out of twelve teenagers they confirm becomes an adult communicant. The difference is that in Unitarian Universalist churches we intentionally raise our children to make their own adult religious choices. Many do stay with us. But others do not. Our congregations are too thinly scattered and our young people too mobile and flexible for us to keep them all.

Of several teens in my high school group some fifteen years ago, one is in Thailand, working for Planned Parenthood International. His bride-to-be, I am told, is Buddhist. Another is in Tennessee, married to a solid young Baptist. They are raising their children as liberal Baptists. A third is in New Jersey, married to an orthodox Jew. They are raising their children in that tradition. Several are still very active in Unitarian Universalist congregations. One chairs the adult religious education committee in his. Another, with a devout Catholic husband, serves on the board of her local UU Fellowship. One is in our young adult group at All Souls in New York. Although I have lost track of many of them, nearly everyone from the group I am still in touch with seems to be spiritually engaged and yet open to the process of religious and ethical dialogue in life. And what more can we hope for, either for our children or for ourselves?

I like what Martin Buber once said: "Everyone— thinker, politician, worker, teacher, lover—may live the life of dialogue, respond to the immediate demands of every hour, and in this dedicated life of I-Thou response and responsibility, you are reaching out and being addressed by God. The rest you can, and must, leave to God's gracious care, for God does not leave this creation forsaken."

PART 4

Jewish and Christian teachings which call us to respond to God's love by loving our neighbors as ourselves.

7

Neighborhood

Forrest Church

A rabbi spoke with God about heaven and hell. "I will show you hell," God said, and they went into a room which had a large pot of stew in the middle. The smell was delicious, but around the pot sat people who were famished and desperate. All were holding spoons with very long handles which reached to the pot, but because the handles of the spoons were longer than their arms, it was impossible to get the stew back into their mouths. "Now I will show you heaven," God said, and they went into an identical room. There was a similar pot of stew, and the people had identical spoons, but they were well nourished and happy. "It's simple," God said. "You see, they have learned to feed one another."

—*Medieval Jewish story*

Jesus is a multidimensional figure. He stands in the prophetic line of Judaism, and for those who would be his followers, he opens up the rich tradition of the Hebrew Scriptures. . . . The words and deeds of Jesus recorded in the New Testament provide the blueprint for human fulfillment. Jesus calls us to comfort and sustain one another, to lift the burdens of the oppressed, and to serve God with joy.

—*Judith L. Hoehler, Unitarian Universalist minister*

IN HIS NOVEL *The Europeans,* Henry James describes an English baroness's first visit to the house of her American cousins in Boston:

> Her glance fell upon young Mr. Brand, who stood there with his arms folded and his hands on his chin, looking at her.
>
> "The Gentleman, I suppose, is a sort of ecclesiastic," she said to Mr. Wentworth, lowering her voice a little.
>
> "He is a minister," answered Mr. Wentworth.
>
> "A Protestant?" asked Eugenia.
>
> "I am a Unitarian, Madam," replied Mr. Brand, impressively.
>
> "Ah, I see," said Eugenia. "Something new."

Mr. Brand is clearly a bit of a stick. He would have benefitted from G. K. Chesterton's reminder, "Angels can fly because they take themselves lightly." A great defender of orthodoxy, Chesterton also insistently pointed out that when it comes to religion novelty is not a particularly strong credential; as often as not, it suggests shortsightedness, impermanence, and faddishness.

On the other hand, hidebound religions, dogmatically fixed to some ancient creed formulated centuries ago in response to theological, political, and sociological conditions of another age and culture, escape the dangers of novelty, but at an unacceptable price. In the 1920s neo-orthodox theologian Karl Barth argued that revelation (the action of the Holy Spirit) was restricted to the sixty-mile stretch between Jerusalem and the Sea of Galilee, and further confined to the short thirty-odd years of Jesus' life. Not only did Barth hold that revelation was sealed from then on, but also that the ancient scriptures preparing for and chronicling the revelation of Jesus Christ constitute our only way to understand the meaning of life and death. Despite the "neo-" in its moniker, there was nothing particularly novel in this point of view. In fact, it was little more than a reprise of the arguments that William Ellery Channing had so eloquently countered a century before when he delivered his famous Baltimore sermon, "Unitarian Christianity."

Preached at the ordination of Jared Sparks in 1819, Channing's sermon was published and reprinted seven times, and became the most popular pamphlet in America since Thomas Paine's *Common Sense*. Not only did he defend the principle of God's unity (rejecting the trinity as nonscriptural), but he also presented contemporary Unitarian views on the interpretation of scripture. "We feel it our bounden duty to exercise our reason upon it perpetually; to compare, to infer, to look beyond the letter to the spirit, to seek in the nature of the subject, and the aim of the writer, his [or her] true meaning; and, in general, to make use of what is known for explaining what is difficult, and for discovering new truths."

Channing's was a quest not for novelty, but for essence. His defense of Unitarianism was also a defense of the Bible and of religion. He recoiled against "the contemptuous manner in which human reason is often spoken of by our adversaries, because it leads, we believe, to universal skepticism." His words remain important even today, because fundamentalism of the right has its whiplash in fundamentalism of the left. When the true believer proclaims that the Bible is the unique word of God—to be accepted without question—the true unbeliever responds by dismissing scripture as a figment of demented imaginations.

A handful of Unitarian Universalists boast that in their church the only time the words "Jesus Christ" are uttered during worship is when their minister trips on the steps. Channing would have found them as unreasonable as those in his day who read their Bibles without thinking. To him the Bible was written not by God, but by inspired people, drawing from both history and experience, who sought to understand better the larger meaning of life and death. Fundamentalists may trivialize the Bible by excluding reason as the principal tool by which it may be understood, but this does not mean that reasonable reflections upon the stories and teachings contained therein cannot markedly advance our own humble search for meaning and for faith.

In addition to William Ellery Channing, another Bostonian who had something new to say about religion was Theodore Parker. In his great sermon, "The Transient and the Permanent in Christianity," Parker offered a dynamic resolution for those of us who wish to mine the Bible for its wisdom without sacrificing our critical faculties. Much of what the Bible contains is time-bound, he argued, and therefore of marginal relevance to us today. But it also contains eternal truths, which we may mine without ever exhausting. "The solar system as it exists in fact is permanent," Parker wrote, "though the notions of Thales and Ptolemy, of Copernicus and Descartes, about this system, prove transient, imperfect approximations to the true expression. So the Christianity of Jesus is permanent, though what passes for Christianity with popes and catechisms, with sects and churches, in the first century or in the nineteenth century, prove transient also."

In defining the permanent in Christianity, Parker went to the heart of Jesus' own teachings. Speaking not as a Christian but as a Jew, Jesus taught his disciples that the Hebrew scriptures could be summarized in two great commandments: "You shall love the Lord your God with all our heart, and with all your soul, and with all your mind. This is the great and first commandment. And a second is like it, You shall love your neighbor as yourself. On these two command- ments depend all the law and the prophets" (Matt. 22:37–40). Drawing his own truth from this succinct summation, Parker concluded that:

> The end of Christianity seems to be to make all [people] one with God as Christ was one with [God]; to bring them to such a state of obedience and goodness that we shall think divine thoughts and feel divine senti- ments, and so keep the law of God by living a life of truth and love. Its means are purity and prayer; getting strength from God, and using it for our [sisters and brothers] as well as ourselves. It allows perfect freedom. It does not demand all [people] to think alike, but to think uprightly, and get as near as possible at truth; not all [people] to live alike, but to live holy, and get as near as possible to a life perfectly divine.

At the turn of the century, when Henry James was writing *The Europeans,* one clever dismissal of Unitar- ians was that we believed in "the fatherhood of God, the brotherhood of man, and the neighborhood of Bos- ton." As with all such caricatures—witness Mr. Brand—this one contained just enough truth to win an honest laugh. But as Channing's and Parker's sermons indicate, far from restricting the action of the Holy Spirit to a sixty-mile stretch between Concord and Cape Cod, nineteenth-century Unitarian and Universalist theologians had in fact liberated the Spirit from her Christian captors.

One could go even further and boast that they adapted the wag's dismissal of Unitarian belief to correspond directly to Jesus' teachings. Uniting the three parts, Channing and Parker preached what Unitarian Universalists have been proclaiming ever since. We believe in "neighborhood"—the universal spirit of neighborliness expressed in those Jewish and Christian teachings which call us to respond to God's love by loving our neighbors as ourselves. It is the fourth source of our common faith.

In the Bible, when religion is defined, its requirements entail concrete duties, not abstract theological formulations. "What does the Lord require of you," the prophet Micah asked, "but to do justice, love mercy, and walk humbly with your God." That is as abstract and theological as it gets. According to Isaiah, our religious charge is even more specific: "to loose the bands of wickedness, to undo the thongs of the yoke, to let the oppressed go free, and to break every yoke . . . to share your bread with the hungry, and bring the homeless poor into your house; when you see the naked, to cover him. . . . If you pour yourself out for the hungry and satisfy the desire of the afflicted, then shall your light rise in the darkness, and your gloom be as the noonday" (Isa. 58:6–10). In the same spirit, Jesus proclaimed to his disciples just before his death, that on the day of judgment the sheep will be separated from the goats by a simple religious quiz: "Did you feed the hungry?" "Did you offer refreshment to the thirsty?" "Did you clothe the naked?" and "Did you visit the sick and those in prison?" (Matt. 25:31–46). And in the New Testament epistles, not only does James—who believed that faith without works is dead—write, "Religion that is pure and undefiled before God . . . is this: to visit orphans and widows in their affliction" (James 1:27), but Paul—who claimed in his letter to Rome that we could be justified by faith alone, and not by works—also places neighborly love at the center of his ethical teachings. In the same letter Paul writes:

> Love one another with brotherly [and sisterly] affection . . . practice hospitality. . . . Bless those who persecute you; bless and do not curse them. Rejoice with those who rejoice, weep with those who weep. Live in harmony with one another; do not be haughty, but associate with the lowly; never be conceited. Repay no one evil for evil, but take thought for what is noble in the sight of all. If possible, so far as it depends upon you, live peaceably with all. Beloved, never avenge yourselves. . . . No, if your [enemies are] hungry, feed

[them]; if [they are] thirsty, give [them] drink. . . . Do not be overcome by evil, but overcome evil with good. (Rom. 12:10–21)

If you look up this passage you will notice that I left out one quote and part of another, each a citation by Paul from the Hebrew scriptures: "Vengeance is mine, I will repay, says the Lord" (Lev. 19:18); and, "If your [enemies are] hungry, feed [them]; if [they are] thirsty, give [them] drink; for by so doing you will heap burning coals upon [their] head" (Prov. 25:21–22). Like many other Unitarian Universalists, I mine the Bible for that which inspires me to be a better person, more loving, more neighborly. It is rich in such material. But the Bible is not a single, sacrosanct book; it is a whole library of books representing the history, legends, laws, wisdom, and poetry of a people. And even these have been edited and re-edited over the centuries; some are of lesser intrinsic interest, more dated by historical context and theological circumstance, than others; some are dramatically uneven in spiritual quality, the most sublime sentiments coupled with theological and ethical barbarisms in the same text. Thus, in drawing inspiration from scriptural teachings as one of the sources of our faith, most Unitarian Universalists approach them more critically than do some orthodox Christians and Jews. Biblical literalists claim that the Bible is the transcript of God's word; biblical humanists are more likely to look beyond the letter to the spirit—the spirit of neighborliness, of kinship, of love.

Almost everyone, even the literal-minded Christian, edits the Bible by focusing on certain passages. Martin Luther hated the Epistle of James, calling it "the straw epistle." And surely not all, but some modern day fundamentalists are quick to cite God's vengeance when quoting scripture. They appear to delight in heaping burning coals, while remaining deaf to the injunctions of Micah, Isaiah, Jesus, and Paul to love and serve, to feed, clothe, and shelter our neighbor. This too represents a selective approach to the Bible, distorting its essence accordingly.

To give but one example of these differences, consider the AIDS crisis. On the one side, the lessons to be drawn from the alarming spread of the deadly AIDS virus—surely not by all, but by some prominent biblical literalists—are these: (1) homosexuality (not to mention drug abuse) is a sin; (2) we know it is a sin because the Bible tells us so; (3) the Bible also tells us that God punishes sinners, that "the wages of sin are death"; therefore (4) the AIDS epidemic is an act of God punishing certain sinners for their evil ways, while dramatically reminding the rest of us of the mortal dangers that accompany sin.

The response of biblical humanists tend to be precisely the opposite. First, the great majority of us reject the presumption that homosexuality is a sin. As Diane

D. Stephenson, a lesbian member of the Unitarian Universalist Congregation of Atlanta, writes, "My religious experience as a Unitarian Universalist for 20 years has sustained me in making critical decisions in my life. My church has always supported me as a person—my sexual orientation has made no difference." Her experience is not unique. On the contrary, no denomination has been more forward in its affirmation of gay and lesbian rights.

Beyond regard for one's sexual orientation and drawing upon the two commandments which summarize all the law and the prophets, biblical humanists place at the center of their response loving our neighbor as ourselves. Our logic proceeds as follows: (1) people with AIDS are our neighbors; (2) our neighbors with AIDS, whether homosexual or heterosexual, are not the enemy, the disease is the enemy; thus (3) our challenge is first, to fulfill the rule of hospitality and the commandment of neighborliness—to care for people with AIDS, to visit and succor them, and to fight for their rights as an oppressed population—and second, to invest our fullest corporate energy unstintingly to find a cure for this dread disease.

In many Unitarian Universalist churches and fellowships, in addition to ministries specifically for people with AIDS and educational programs to help abate our own members' unfounded fear of contagion from incidental contact, we also witness to the principles of our liberal faith in the larger community. The University Unitarian Church in Seattle has purchased a seven-bedroom house in the city's Capital Hill area, converted it into a shelter for AIDS patients, and named it "The Mark DeWolfe House" in honor of the Reverend Mark DeWolfe, a Unitarian Univeralist minister who died of AIDS. As their minister, Peter Raible, said, "This is an opportunity for our church to assume a leading role, both in meeting this basic human need, and in acting to affirm human dignity." He later added, "How much better we are when we do something concrete, something beyond sweatshirt theology!" In the same spirit, The Unitarian Church of All Souls in New York sponsored an extensive advertising campaign, first run in local city busses and subway cars, and now being extended across the country by other Unitarian Universalist congregations. The messages we are sending out are clear: "Treat a person with AIDS with kindness: It won't kill you." "AIDS is a human disease, and demands a humane response." "AIDS: the more you understand, the more understanding you'll be." These two local efforts, together with the work of AIDS task forces in churches and fellowships throughout the denomination, emblematically capture the essence of our fourth source: Jewish and Christian teachings which call us to respond to God's love by loving our neighbors as ourselves.

We are not alone in applying these teachings as best we can in our response to AIDS and in our ministries to people with AIDS. Many Christians also respond as we do, drawing inspiration from the teachings of love that they find in the Bible rather than those of vengeance. Mother Teresa once said of people with AIDS, "Each of them is Jesus in distressing disguise." She remembers when Jesus said, "I was sick and you visited me. . . . Truly, I say to you, as you did it to one of the least of these my brethren, you did it to me." (Matt. 25:35–40).

Some Unitarian Universalists, who still suffer from a religious education based upon teachings from the Bible that inspired fear rather than love in their hearts, have little desire to return to the Bible and reclaim its essential teachings as a part of their own faith. Others, Unitarian Universalist Christians, center their faith and their devotions on the scriptures. But however we gauge the nature of the Bible's authority, nearly all of us can embrace the principle of neighborliness at the heart of the Judeo-Christian tradition.

Aspiring to appropriate the spirit of the love commandment, I have developed a healthy appreciation for paradox, the ethical paradox. Give and you shall receive; empty yourself and you shall be filled; lose yourself and be found. Every sacrifice (the word means to render sacred), every work of love, or selfless deed of praise, is redemptive both for ourselves and for others. Instead of feeling overwhelmed by a sense of insignificance and powerlessness, we lose ourselves, together with our ineffectual fretfulness, in the concrete work of the commonwealth of God, the work of justice being done and love being shared, the work of healing and wholeness, the saving work. Something powerful is at work here, akin to the proverbial planting of a mustard seed, yielding well beyond anything that might be measured in terms of self-gratification on a quid pro quo basis. In the words of Jesus, "the measure you give will be the measure you set, and still more will be given you" (Mark 4:24).

If the ethical paradox, and its fruit of neighborliness, is evident throughout the scriptures, nowhere is it more eloquently expressed than in the Beatitudes of Jesus (Matt. 5:3–12). With these, therefore (using my own free translation), I close this discussion of the fourth source of our living faith.

Blessed are the poor in spirit, for they know the unutterable beauty of simple things.

Blessed are those who mourn, for they have dared to risk their hearts by giving of their love.

Blessed are the meek, for the gentle earth shall embrace them and hallow them as its own.

Blessed are those who hunger and thirst for right-eousness, for they shall know the taste of noble thoughts and deeds.

Blessed are the merciful, for in return theirs is the gift of giving.

Blessed are the pure in heart, for they shall be at one with themselves and the universe.

Blessed are the peacemakers, for theirs is a kinship with everything that is holy.

Blessed are those who are persecuted for right-eousness' sake, for the truth will set them free.

8

Expectations

John A. Buehrens

The bond of unity in a church is not a shared belief but a shared worship. Worship (worth-ship) is an act of reverence for what is regarded as of great, or supreme, worth. In the ultimate analysis this is but another way of capturing the real meaning of love. What is of real worth to us, in the full sense, we cannot help but love. Love is reverence for life, to use Albert Schweitzer's phrase, and reverence is a mode of worship. Worship in a Unitarian setting becomes a shared act of celebration expressing our love for things of worth— those values by which and for which we live, in whatever picture-language they may be symbolized.
—*Phillip Hewett, Canadian Unitarian minister*

To be perfect is impossible. God forgives our imperfections because we were created that way. It's all right to be human.
—*Marjorie Newlin Leaming, Universalist minister*

WHENEVER THE MAJOR religious holidays of our culture roll around, I am reminded that Jewish and Christian teachings are not only about love. They are also about our expectations. We expect holidays. We look forward to them. They come in a regular cycle, seemingly as natural and universal as the seasons themselves. For a culture that took its shape in the northern hemisphere, winter holidays of light, Christmas and Hanukkah, are quite predictable. So are holidays in spring that symbolize new life, Passover and Easter. What should surprise us, far more than it does, is that we celebrate these holidays, and not others.

In the Roman world two thousand years ago, Christianity and rabbinic Judaism were minor religious movements. Both were sects that emerged from a marginal people at the edge of the empire, a people who were thinly scattered, and with few prospects for anything but persecution, especially after the destruction of the Jerusalem temple (in the year 70 of the Common Era). There were hundreds of other faiths, cults, and cultural movements. Many were more popular and consequently more influential.

Several of the ancient competitors of Judaism and Christianity have some fascinating analogues today. The cult of Asclepius, the god of health, corresponds to our modern "religion" of health foods, exercise, and various forms of healing and therapy. The veneration of the Roman gods finds its equivalent in the civil religion of modern imperial patriotism. Roman fascination with the religions of Egypt and the Orient continues in the modern interest in Eastern religions.

Current debates among academics have parallels in the various schools of ancient philosophy (Platonists, Cynics, Stoics, and Epicureans). Such competitors of Judaism and Christianity have not disappeared. Yet the chief holidays we celebrate are Christmas and Hanukkah, Passover and Easter. Some hints about the power of Jewish and Christian teachings may lie in these holidays themselves.

The seasons may return with regularity, but these holidays do not simply celebrate the cycles of time. Instead, they tell stories about unexpected turns in human history. They express a form of faith that dares to reflect on human expectations being upset.

For example, in the Hanukkah story, the Syrians expect to impose their king's decree that his image be worshiped by everyone, including the Jews. Instead, Judah the Maccabee and his band of fighters prevail against them. Then, even the victor's expectations are confounded. The temple is cleansed and the eternal flame rekindled, and the oil thought sufficient for only one day burns unaccountably for the required eight.

In the Christmas story, a man named Joseph has his expectations about the young woman who is to be his wife upset by her pregnancy. Yet he does not abandon her. He stays beside her, a manifestation of unconditional love. Their child is born in humble obscurity, but goes on to have an unexpected, indeed, world-historical, impact.

In the Easter story, the followers of Jesus expect him to be enthroned as king. Instead, he meets a humiliating death. His disciples scatter in fear and despair. But on the third day, his tomb, unexpectedly, is reported empty. Those who loved him begin to see him again and to sense that the person who made them feel so close to God and to one another when in his presence is not dead after all, but somehow resurrected. His spirit goes before them into Galilee, and is said to be present wherever two or three gather in his name.

And at Passover, the oldest story of all is told—again about expectations overturned. "It would have been enough [*Dayenu*]," we sing around the Seder table, if the children of Israel had simply been freed from Egyptian bondage—but to be given the Torah, and then led into the land of promise! A favorite *midrash* on the Passover story says that when Moses asked the Red Sea to part, at first nothing happened; the sea only parted when one of the Hebrews had faith enough to defy expectations and actually enter the water.

Isn't it ironic that sometimes we define "an act of God" as insurance lawyers do ("something that no rational person could have expected"), while other times talk about God only makes sense when things are ordered and beautiful, as in the glory of nature's cycles. The Jewish and Christian holidays remind us to find the mark of God less in the regularities of nature than in the unexpected turns that life can take, in the humbling of the arrogant and the uplifting of the lowly. They proclaim that both the realm of nature and the realm of history are part of a larger realm— the commonwealth of God.

Luther once called the whole universe "God's masquerade," in which God seems to hide from us while "ruling so strangely by making a hubbub." What does it mean to trust or love a God who works by upsetting our human expectations? Most of us would prefer to believe in something far simpler—in a cosmic moralist, for example, whose moral order would allow us to make confident judgments about who is good and who is bad. But as often as not, life confounds our expectations.

One August Sunday in Knoxville, Tennessee, I worshiped at the First Baptist Church, smugly expecting something I could scoff at. Instead, the simple yet profound message sounded again and again. It was based, amazingly enough, upon an old Unitarian hymn: "Watchman, tell us of the night / What its signs of promise are." The other hymns, readings, and anthems from Isaiah, the Psalms, and the Gospels all spoke of standing vigil, being watchful. The minister looked out on the large congregation and told us in short, "Friends, you *think* you know where the dawn is going to come. You think you know what God's gonna do. But you don't. Every time you see something new on the horizon, something that's different, that's new, you say, 'Why, that's against God; that's against the Bible.' Don't you?" (There were nods of self-recognition all around.) "Well, maybe it is and maybe it isn't. Maybe God is just fixing to surprise you, to upset your expectations. God's done it before and may do it again. Not all dawns come in the east. God may be making a new heaven and new earth. Don't be so quick to condemn everything new."

I returned home saying to Unitarian Universalists who complained to me about the Baptist fundamentalists all around them, "Well, there are Baptists—and then there are Baptists." I returned far more aware of the smugness of my own expectations as well. Not that any of us enjoy having our expectations overturned, but some deep lessons about what it means to love our neighbors (much less to love God) may be hidden in such events.

I remember, for example, the first holiday that Gwen and I celebrated together as a married couple. It came close to being a complete disaster, not because of any differences in our theology but because of different expectations. It was Thanksgiving—that most inclusive of American holidays. From my point of view there was too much of everything: too many guests (her family, my family, her friends, my friends); too much food (her mother's recipes, my mother's recipes); and too much fuss altogether. From Gwen's vantage point, the problem was not too much, but too little. An important moment to her was omitted, and I was to blame.

I had been asked to carve, something I had never done before, but I was willing. I put on an apron, entered the kitchen, and attacked the bird with as much artistry as I could muster. And what reward did I get? Gwen burst into tears. In *her* family, the turkey is brought to the *table,* laid before the *paterfamilias,* grace is said, and *then* he carves. "So I fail patriarchy," I hollered later. "What do you expect?"

This story is more than a parable about sex roles or family traditions. It points to a deep rift in the human psyche. There *is* too much of everything—more than we ever expected as children. As adults, we can feel overwhelmed. There are too many galaxies, too many light-years, too much space, and too many *things;* too many stars, too many creatures, too many people, problems, and choices; too much entirely on the table; too many nations, cultures, and religions; too many species of plants and animals—certainly too many insects, bacteria, and viruses altogether. Wouldn't it have been better if God had been more moderate and modest in the work of creation? Why couldn't there have been, say, just *one* language, culture, and religion among humans? Wouldn't that have made for less conflict? What was God trying to do in creating all this seemingly senseless superabundance? Showing off?

Nonetheless, at times we all feel deprived. There's not too much in life; there's something missing. We feel alone and disappointed, with people and the state of the universe in general, and how we are treated in particular.

"Sometimes I'd like to ask God why He [*sic*] created the Universe with so much poverty, hunger, and misery when He could have done something about it," begins a current cartoon.

"Well, why don't you?" someone asks in the second panel.

"Because I'm afraid that God might ask *me* the same question."

The something missing may be you, it may be me. "God is not here or there, to be possessed," said Martin Buber, "but is everywhere, to be met. It is only *we* who are not always there."

Good ministers know that our vocation does not consist solely in meeting the expectations of other people, however it may begin there. As my wife says, "The first task in the ministry is to help people feel safe; then the real work can start." But the real "work" of growing together religiously consists above all else of learning to behave well, to respond creatively even when our expectations in life are disappointed.

According to legend, one of our most creative ministers, after nearly twenty years, became depressed about a slump in congregational energies and simply stayed home one Sunday morning. When eleven o'clock arrived and no minister had appeared, the congregation practiced good Emersonian self-reliance and began to fashion their own worship, while a small group of leaders called at the parsonage to see what was amiss.

"Are you ill?" they asked.

"No."

"Well, then, are you coming?"

"If you wish," the minister replied, "but I'm a little surprised to see that you want anyone to come. The way attendance has been, and the apathy about the church school, and the building, and the financial drive, not to mention our social ministries, I felt the need to test whether anyone was still interested at all."

I do not recommend this ministerial tactic. But good people of faith know that the purpose of ministry is not necessarily to fulfill expectations. Early in his ministry, John Wolf, now the minister of one of our largest congregations, All Souls Unitarian Church in Tulsa, Oklahoma, was interviewed by a ministerial search committee. After awhile they said, "We like you very much. We'd like you to be our minister. But there's just one thing we don't understand. Unitarian Universalist ministers are generally thought to come in two varieties: humanist and theist. Which are you?"

"That depends," said Wolf.

Shocked by such blatant opportunism, one of the committee members asked, "What on earth do you mean?"

"That depends on you," John replied. "If you folks are theists, then I'm a humanist. But if you're humanists, then I'm a theist."

This wasn't just an attempt to avoid a new job. It was good theology. My teacher Harvey Cox might have called it a "theology of juxtaposition," running the rasp against the grain. When people take pride in trusting God, then the prophetic thing is to test what difference that makes in their day-to-day treatment of other human beings. When they pride themselves too much on being ethical and humanistic, then perhaps they need reminding that the long-term capacity to embrace the second great commandment—to love one's neighbor—depends on the depth of our ability to live out the first—to love the Ground of Being with all of one's heart and mind and strength.

I once led a weekend retreat devoted to exploring how the horizontal dimension of religion is related to the vertical, the ethical to the inward and spiritual. I left free time for reading, reflection, and recreation between my four brief meditative talks. The first talk was an invitation to reach inward, cultivating an inner life that does not eliminate loneliness, but converts it to a deeper capacity for spirituality and receptive solitude. The second stressed the importance of reaching out, converting defensiveness and hostility into hospitality—the spiritual capacity to make room in one's life for the presence of others. The third advocated joining with others to help make this world a more hospitable and home-like place, finding disciplined ways to grow spiritually through acts of service. The fourth dealt with worship, personal and corporate—reaching toward the transcendent. We closed the retreat with a Sunday morning service that the group itself designed—a modified Quaker meeting, in which silence upheld the readings, prayers, and personal reflections which people shared.

Toward the end of the service, one participant revealed that late the first evening a friend he had persuaded to come along had said, "This retreat isn't meeting my expectations; I'm going home." Precisely what was wrong wasn't clear. Too casual? Too traditional? Who could be sure?

"This weekend didn't meet my expectations either," he said. "It changed them: my expectations of myself, of other people, of helping, of worship. I'm more aware of pain than I was before, but also of grace—in the world, in sharing, in silence, in working and worshiping together. I'm glad I came and even more glad I stayed."

When people ask, "What can I expect from an association with the Unitarian Universalists?" I respond, "Whatever expectations you bring, expect to have them upset by us, at least in part." After all, some of our people are quite unconventional. And yet others may seem shockingly traditional to be part of such a supposedly avant-garde movement. The same is true of our congregations. If you do not want anything to change in your life, it might be safer by far to stay away. Over the years, I have been disappointed at times, but more often it has been my *low* expectations of people that have been upset. I have seen obstinate atheists develop a sense of transcendence, conservative pietists develop a social conscience, cynics begin to pray, and skeptics begin to articulate what they *do* believe. Above all, through association with our free faith, I have seen people grow unexpectedly in their capacity to love, to feel and respond creatively to both the pain and the grace in human living.

The meeting place may be a white church on the village green or a rented room in a suburban Y; a Gothic cathedral or a modern structure by Frank Lloyd Wright—or a blend of the two, like the First and Second Church in Boston. It may be a large congregation with several ministers, or a small lay-led fellowship where everyone knows that they are the ministers, one to another. The setting may be a college town or an inner city. The people may be predominantly white or multi-ethnic, rich or poor. Gay men and lesbian women may be either open or quietly present among them. The music may consist of professional choir plus organ and a brass quintet, or a single volunteer playing a guitar. The speaker may be a minister, a distinguished guest, or an ordinary member. The order of service may include scripture, hymns, prayers, sermon, and benediction (the pattern that goes back to ancient synagogues), or it may omit any or all of these features and be created especially for a particular Sunday. As one of our denominational leaders, Joan Goodwin, says, "Our Unitarian Universalist congregations are as unique as fingerprints, and as similar." Among the things you can count on in a Unitarian Universalist community, regardless of size, theological character, or institutional form, is that sooner or later your expectations will be upset.

Our worship may vary widely in form and theology, but for Unitarian Universalist gatherings to be effective, worship must reach out and stretch us in several different directions. Good worship will strive for *height*. It should be a "celebration of life," to use the favorite definition of worship of the late Unitarian minister Von Ogden Vogt. Making a joyful noise (even if the hymn is unfamiliar) and reaffirming the goodness of being are important aspects of all true worship. But authentic worship also has *depth*. That is, it has a meditative dimension—acknowledging among us the brokenness and grief, the estrangement and remorse. In the horizontal dimension, worship needs to have *breadth* to be inclusive. That means more than simply using gender-inclusive language (as important as we take that to be), more than remembering to mourn with those who mourn as well as rejoice with those who rejoice. It means using simple, familiar forms that will set newcomers at ease, rather than puzzling them with unfamiliar rituals or patterns of communication. By no means does this breadth require a sacrifice of all sense of tradition. On the contrary, we must gratefully acknowledge our debt to the past. We have arrived where we are because of all that lies *behind* us. Finally, effective worship asks us to stretch *forward*. It has a dimension of aspiration.

The balance takes integrity to maintain. As a young minister I once told my congregation that I was learning to be less concerned with pleasing them as they sat before me. Often that had weakened our worship in some dimension because I strove to avoid "too much" exuberance, tradition, or aspiration. Instead, I was learning to be conscious of what stood *behind* me when I faced them in the pulpit. Call it "the great tradition," or the God of our forebears—most ministers have a sense that if we ever turned around while up there preaching, we'd run the risk of being struck dead!

With all the different dimensions of worship, it is no wonder that not every service is equally satisfying at every moment. We do not always get what we expect or want. From week to week, we come with differing human needs and expectations, for celebration, meditation, inclusion, tradition, and aspiration. What is amazing is that we so often get at least something of what we need.

The Roman Catholic writer Flannery O'Connor once wrote a letter to her friend Cecil Dawkins, who had expressed dissatisfaction with all forms of organized religion and may have expected sympathy. O'Connor didn't offer much. "It is easy for any child to pick out the faults in the sermon on his [or her] way home from Church every Sunday," she told him. "It is impossible for him to find out the hidden love that makes a person, in spite of intellectual limitations, neuroticism, and lack of strength, give one's life to the service of God's people, however bumblingly one may go about it." She told him that behind his complaining lay an inadequate understanding of sin; that what he was asking for was nothing short of the kingdom of heaven realized on earth. "Christ was crucified on earth and the Church is crucified . . . by all of us," she wrote, "by her members most particularly, because She is a church of sinners."

"You don't serve God by saying: the Church is ineffective, I'll have none of it," O'Connor added. "Your pain at its lack of effectiveness is a sign of your nearness to God. We [can] help overcome this lack of effectiveness . . . [but] to have the Church be what you want it to be would require the continuous miraculous meddling of God in human affairs, whereas it is our dignity that we are allowed more or less to get on with those graces that come through faith . . . and which work through our human nature. God has chosen to operate in this manner. We can't understand this but we can't reject it without rejecting life." "To expect too much," she concluded, "is to have a sentimental view of life; and this is a softness which ends in bitterness. Charity is hard and endures."

Many of our problems with religion and life come from confusions about love, human and divine. We expect from finite, conditioned human beings an unconditional love. But even our loved ones cannot always respond unconditionally. They are not divine. They are only our spouses, friends, children, or parents. By the same token, our culture's tradition of thinking of God as a parent can lead us into thinking that if we please God, lead a good life, avoid temptations, then God will reward us. But the truth is that this is only an image of God—and a conditioned one at that. The real God is unconditioned, transcendent, and sends sunlight and rain on the just and the unjust alike. Within all life's changes and upsets we may discover something gracious, something very much like love. But it is a hard and enduring love, indiscriminate in overturning our more personal, temporary, and narrow expectations.

We all have expectations. We look outward through a little chink in our armor, one conditioned by our background, our experience, our doubts, and our faith. The true ground of our hope is not in our expectations, however, no matter how grand or how humble. It lies in the hubbub, which upsets our expectations and reorders our perceptions. We are constantly being challenged therefore to become more inclusive, mature, and enduring in our love.

I will not offer the cynic's advice, "Blessed are those who expect nothing, for they shall never be disappointed," but I will tell all those who approach our churches and fellowships that the dawn may not appear just where you expect: your new religious community will not always fill your every desire; on the other hand, you may perhaps find, almost certainly in unexpected ways, something of what you truly need.

The last chapter ended with a new version of the Beatitudes. These are my blessings for those who join us on the pilgrimage of faith we have chosen and come to love, in Unitarian Universalism.

Blessed are those who yearn for deepening more than escape; who can renounce smugness and be shaken in conscience; who are not afraid to grow in spirit.

Blessed are those who take seriously the bonds of community; who regularly join in celebration and learning; who come to church on time, and never let mere weather or inertia keep them home; who come as much to minister as to be ministered unto.

Blessed are those who bring—not send—their children; who invite their friends to come along, to join in fellowship, service, learning, and growth.

Blessed are those who know that the work of the church is the transformation of society; who have a vision of Beloved Community transcending the present, and who do not shrink from controversy, sacrifice, or change.

Blessed are those who support the church and its work by their regular, sustained and generous giving; and who give of themselves no less than their money.

Blessed are those who know that the church is often imperfect, even inadequate, yet rather than harbor feelings of anger or personal disappointment, bring their concerns and needs to the attention of the church, its ministers, and leaders.

Blessed are those who when asked to serve, do it gladly; who realize that change is brought about through human meeting, and who do the dull work of committees, and stay till the end.

Blessed are those who speak their minds in meetings, who can take and give criticism; who keep alive their sense of humor.

Blessed are they indeed.

PART 5

*Humanist teachings which counsel us to heed the
guidance of reason and the results of science, and
warn us against idolatries of the mind and spirit.*

9

Beyond Idolatry

Forrest Church

Long long ago, it seemed so simple. The universe was a three-storied apartment house, with heaven on the top floor, full of gods and stars; earth in the middle, full of people and animals and plants; and hell in the basement, full of terrible and scary things. God had nothing else to do but sit up there watching us. We were the center of attention. We were his people.

Then came Copernicus. He said that the sun did not move around the earth at all, but was a fixed star. He said it was the earth and us on it that did the moving, and, worse, that the earth was just one of the planets that so moved, one among many, and not at the center of anything at all. . . .

In the last few decades we have been entering a new vision of the universe as radical and revolutionary as the Copernican changeover, and we still have not worked out what it all means, either in theology or in our view of what humanity is and what we ought to do with our lives.

—Judith Walker-Riggs, Unitarian Universalist minister

SOME YEARS AGO, I was engaged in a running battle with my children concerning good manners, those little lubricants of sociability that grease the wheels of polite society. I do not mean advanced good manners, not "Good morning, Sir," just "Good morning"; not "Thank you very much, Ma'am," just simply "Thanks." I'm talking about "Hello," "Good-bye," "Please," that sort of thing. To judge from my children, you would have thought that these simple, happy, agreeable little words were fishbones; they almost never failed to stick in their throats.

One morning, after a particularly excruciating exchange on this subject, I blew up. Certainly not because my children had become a source of daily embarrassment to me—certainly not that—but rather because, like any good father, I considered myself obliged to instruct them in the ways of the world.

"Daddy," my son said, "you don't always have good manners."

I had to admit that was true.

"And Mommy doesn't always have good manners, either."

He was right again.

"Even God doesn't have good manners," he triumphantly proclaimed. This left me speechless.

"What do you mean God doesn't have good manners?" I finally asked.

"Daddy," my son explained, "if God is inside us,

then God *makes* us not say 'Please' and 'Thank you.'"

How do you figure it? After years of exposure to the free spirit of Unitarian Universalism, my son sounded like a Calvinist.

Now that he's in college, it's time for me to introduce him to *The Humanist Manifesto*. In 1933, a group of religious humanists, most of whom were from the Chicago area and many of whom were Unitarian, together composed a brief document outlining the basic principles of humanism. It was not designed as an anti-religious statement, but as a testament to the religious spirit as it might best be expressed in our own time. "The time has come for widespread recognition of the radical changes in religious beliefs throughout the modern world," it began. "The time is past for mere revision of traditional attitudes. Science and economic change have disrupted the old beliefs. Religions the world over are under the necessity of coming to terms with new conditions created by a vastly increased knowledge and experience. In every field of human activity, the vital movement is now in the direction of a candid and explicit humanism."

The word *humanism* is blasphemy to many deeply religious people even today, more than a half a century after this document was composed. It suggests godlessness, sacrilege, and immorality. Yet *The Humanist Manifesto* is a profoundly spiritual document. Yes, it rejects superstition, while calling for the exercise of reason in matters of faith, but it also expresses deep commitment to the commonweal. Far from being antireligious, this manifesto proclaimed, "Today [our] larger understanding of the universe, [our] scientific achievements, and [our] deeper appreciation of [the kinship of all people], have created a situation which requires a new statement of the means and purposes of religion."

In far more important matters than good manners, but in those as well, God doesn't make us do anything; we are responsible for our own destiny, and capable of making it better. "The goal of humanism is a free and universal society in which people voluntarily and intelligently cooperate for the common good," the signers wrote. "Humanists demand a shared life in a shared world. . . . We assert that humanism will: (a) affirm life rather than deny it; (b) seek to elicit the possibilities of life, not flee from it; and, (c) endeavor to establish the conditions of a satisfactory life for all, not merely for a few."

Among the thirty signers were several prominent Unitarian and Universalist ministers, including John Dietrich, Lester Mondale, Curtis Reese, Clinton Lee Scott, and David Rhys Williams. The document was subsequently revised in *The Humanist Manifesto II* (1970) and signed by many Unitarian Universalists. Both statements exemplify our fifth source of faith: the humanist teachings that counsel us to heed the guidance of reason and the results of science, and warn us against the idolatries of the mind and spirit.

The inclusion of a warning against idolatries of the mind and spirit is not an afterthought, it is absolutely critical to the integrity of our faith, protecting even science and rationalism from becoming idols. Rationalism as an idol easily becomes rationalization. Science and technology without awe and humility about how they are used too easily become threats to both nature and humanity, as our nuclear age has shown. Mere freedom from traditional theistic belief does not guarantee just or responsible social behavior. Idolizing such freedom can lead either to self-absorption and "possessive individualism" or to the many idolatries promoted by consumerism and by manipulative would-be messiahs.

James Luther Adams wrote that "idolatry occurs when a social movement adopts as the center of loyalty an idol, a segment of reality torn away from the context of universality, an inflated, misplaced abstraction made into an absolute." Adams lived in Germany during the 1930s. He watched with horror as Nazi propaganda about the greatness of "Deutsche humanismus" coopted many of the most humanistic religious liberals. The only effective religious resistance to the powers and principalities of evil came from neo-orthodox stalwarts such as Karl Barth and the Christian martyr Dietrich Bonhoeffer. Given the dangers of idolatry, it may paradoxically be our very liberal virtues, the things of which we are most proud, that are most likely to betray us.

In his two-volume history of Unitarianism, Earl Morse Wilbur, longtime president of Starr King School in Berkeley, identified freedom, tolerance, and reason as the essential principles that we have espoused in religious life across the centuries. When we turn to our own congregations the question becomes, how do these great principle—when enshrined as idols—work their subtle tyranny and undermine the social effectiveness our faith.

Consider freedom. Is there more than a semantic difference between religious liberalism and liberal religion? Are we liberals who happen to gather in churches or religious people who practice our religion according to liberal principles? Religious liberalism places emphasis upon the substantive—liberalism—reducing religion to a mere adjective. When this happens the dimensions of our faith become modifiers, secondary to an isolated precept, which when abstracted from the whole becomes an idol: the idol of a political ideology or, worse, the idol of "possessive individualism."

Following the precedent of our nineteenth-century forbears, we Unitarian Universalists have come to trust and place great value on freedom and individualism. What we tend to forget is that they emphasized freedom in order to liberate themselves from bondage.

Today our problem is not bondage, but bondlessness. Most of us are already free. We don't need more freedom. We need the resolve to employ the freedom we have responsibly. We need to invest a little of our precious freedom and bond ourselves to others in redemptive community.

Because of our tradition and our self-image as a "faith of the free," some people who come to our churches calling themselves "free-spirits" are hell-bent on fighting the evil of an organized anything. They enter our institutions as fierce individualists, rebellious religious adolescents, champions, above all else, of their precious freedom. Vigilant about protecting themselves from even the slightest restriction, they vigorously censure any word or action, in worship or elsewhere, that might offend their often very brittle and "reactionary" sensibilities. Our real problem is that many of the free spirits who insist on joining our institutions know how to do only one thing when they find themselves within it: they know how to savage it.

If idolized in a like manner, Wilbur's second principle, tolerance, compounds the damage. By one definition, to tolerate means "to bear with repugnance." The problem is that some things and some people's actions are so repugnant that we shouldn't bear with them, and others deserve not merely our tolerance, but our active respect. In our congregations, some people tend to "tolerate" the most dysfunctional members, insisting that in no way should we ever impose our corporate will upon them. But such individuals can destroy our congregations.

Ours is a democratic faith. We acknowledge the concerns of individuals in our churches and act in the spirit of openness and inclusivity as often as possible. But this is only possible when these same people are willing to acknowledge the higher interests of the whole body. Otherwise, they can't play. Why not? Because we need to do more than merely serve them. We have a higher goal, a higher good. When we lose our perspective and honor destructive behavior by permitting it to continue, we become nothing more than this: modern-day Pharisees of freedom and sophists of tolerance.

Wilbur's third principle is reason. When reason is reduced to rationality, it too can become an idol. We lose track of the spirit, even of such documents as *The Humanist Manifesto*, by focusing on the letter. The more legalistic thinkers among us believe that in order to be intellectually legitimate, any opinion we hold, religious or otherwise, must be verifiable as fact. Such people resemble fundamentalists of the right; they are fundamentalists of the left. Such people hold that anything that is not rational is irrational and therefore is to be rejected. A sound reason knows its own limitations. It suggests that beyond the rational lies a transrational realm. We enter it in our dreams; we enter it in moments of worship. We enter it singing, when the tunes are good, even if the words are not. We enter it in lovemaking and dancing and stargazing. We break through to a transrational realm beyond knowing or naming.

By ignoring this reality in a narrow attempt to guard the portals of rationality against all intruders, we betray the teachings of both reason and science (which, together with our rejection of idolatry, comprise the wellspring of our faith's fifth source). Many leading scientists are far ahead in this regard. Recent discoveries in mathematics, cell biology, and quantum physics make no apparent sense, at least not according to the known canons of rationality. In probing the mysteries of the universe and the mind, researchers on the edge of discovery find themselves moving freely between the rational and the transrational realms. The physicist Alan Lightman writes, "Of all people today, I think scientists have the deepest faith in the unseen world. The greater the scientist, the deeper his [or her] faith." Even allowing for hyperbole, where does that leave people who respect science but don't know anything about it? Having traded God for "truth," they are left with neither.

The philosopher and theologian Paul Tillich once said that "the first word of religion must be spoken against religion." When spoken, it is almost always a word of warning against idolatries of the mind and spirit. This is not merely a negative, or critical, function, for it liberates us to heed the guidance of reason and science with open, instead of dogmatically focused, eyes.

Since *The Humanist Manifesto* was written, scientific breakthroughs have dramatically expanded our perspective, both of the universe and of our relationship to it. We have seen stunning pictures from space: the Earth, blue-green and marbled with clouds, rising over the moon's horizon. Never before has the beauty of our ecosystem been more graphically portrayed. New research in biology suggests that life on Earth is far more interdependent and organically related than we might ever have imagined. We are part of one another, not only in a rhetorical and ethical sense—one body, many members—but also in a literal sense. The kinship of all is more than a dream; it is a reality. Not only are all people intimately related, but every living thing on this planet is kin to every other, not so much in a great chain of being, as in an intricate nexus, an interdependent and fragile web.

Breakthroughs in science directly advance our religious understanding, offering new metaphors to help explain the nature of our being. Take the holograph. This is a metaphor drawn from modern technology itself. Biology has shown that each individual shares organically in a complex living system, even as every cell in our body, however distinct in function, carries the genetic coding of the whole being. In a hologram, a three-dimensional image is created by the interplay of two lasers, an object, and a photoplate of thousands of tiny "cells." Incredibly, even if the photoplate is dashed to bits, one can direct the laser beam through any single shard of lens remaining, and the three-dimensional image, however faint, will still appear. Again, the whole is contained in each of the parts. The idea that the earth itself is an organism (sometimes called the Gaia hypothesis) draws on an idea as old as the ancient Stoic humanists, whose emphasis on relatedness can be found in religious thinking from Pauline teaching about "the body of Christ" to an Emersonian emphasis on the individual soul and the Oversoul.

These new metaphors also correspond to the insights of feminist theology, challenging us to move toward a relational ethic based on a principle of cooperation rather than competition. They challenge our traditional individualism, at least in the atomistic sense. We are all individuals, of course, but sovereignty lies in the corporate body, not the individual member. To be loyal to "the highest" in us, we must act with reverence toward all of life. By defining virtue in a cooperative rather than a competitive fashion, we seek the common good, which moves us wherever possible from "either/or" confrontation to "both/and" reconciliation. This is the goal of arms negotiation. It can also be practiced within our homes, offices, and churches, between races and faiths, even between people and their environment.

The original *Humanist Manifesto*, signed by thirty men and no women, was written without benefit of these new, transformational insights into the nature of our shared being. This is not to say that individual signers were not prophetically aware of the new, unfolding vision of reality. As early as 1920, Curtis Reese, then minister of our church in Des Moines, Iowa, summed up liberal religion in this single statement: "Conscious committal and loyalty to worthful causes and goals in order that free and positive personality may be developed, intelligently associated, and cosmically related." He added that "humanistic liberalism constantly aims to promote the widest possible human comradeship and the closest possible human fellowship. And this aim is underwritten by the knowledge that co-operation and not competition is the dominant factor in the growth of the race." Today we might add, "and also to its survival."

With its subtle interplay between reason, science, and resistance to idolatry, the humanist tradition continues to change and grow. As long as we remain true to the humanist spirit, that growth will continue. We will respond to the forces of retrenchment by tapping the transformational power of new models of interdependence and community, which are unfolding in the writings of feminist and liberation theologians, and we will continue to encourage scientific exploration into the nature of our shared being.

In traditional religious language, we have moved from defending (or even attacking) the bastions of the Kingdom of God. Today, our challenge is to codevelop what Dr. King called "the Beloved Community"—the work of love being shared and justice being done in a realm where that which is greater than all is present in each. In that sense, the Beloved Community may also be "the commonwealth of God." According to the level of cooperation we achieve with one another and with that which is in each of us but greater than all of us, we shall either thrive or perish.

What we end up with is please and thank you in spades. Call it metamanners. If God is inside us, our neighbor is inside us as well, not only inside us, but also among us, between us, intertwined with us, never apart. With this new knowledge, our religious challenge is greater than ever. We must employ our reason and the insights of science, mindful of the dangers of idolatry, to increase our understanding and cultivate the garden of the spirit in ways undreamed of before. We must not only nurture a deeper appreciation for the wonder and majesty of life, but renew our sense of responsibility for how the story we are telling will finally turn out.

IO

Mind and Spirit

John A. Buehrens

Far from having nothing to say, religious liberals have to proclaim, over and over again, against both religious and secular adversaries, the good news that the future remains open and the Fates are not in control.

—*Gene Reeves, Unitarian Universalist theologian*

I believe that we are here to some purpose, that the purpose has something to do with the future, and that it transcends altogether the limits of our present knowledge and understanding. If you like, you can call the transcendent purpose God. If it is God, it is a Socinian God, inherent in the universe and growing in power and knowledge as the universe unfolds. Our minds are not only expressions of its purpose but are also contributions to its growth.

—*Freeman Dyson, Infinite in All Directions*

WE ONLY KNOW two things for certain: "I am," and "I will die." Religion is our response. Whether it is spoken or unspoken, conscious or unconscious, inherited or chosen, we all have a religion of some sort or another, for religion is not merely a matter of belief or affiliation. It is a matter of how we chose to live.

The first great certainty is associated with mind, as in Descartes's "I think, therefore I am." The second certainty is associated with spirit, as in Pasternak's novel, *Dr. Zhivago*, when the physician says to a young woman dying of cancer, "Your spirit will live on, you know. Your spirit is you in others, others in you."

Unitarian Universalism aspires to a special form of religious community—one in which individuals are never asked to check their minds at the church door, but in which they offer one another the possibility of rediscovering an authentic and personal spirituality. We remind ourselves that how we live does matter, even after we die. We are related, forever, to one another.

The living tradition we share draws from diverse sources. At the moment we're considering "humanist teachings which counsel us to heed the guidance of reason and the results of science, and warn us against idolatries of the mind and spirit."

Behind all the religious pluralism that enriches and ennobles our faith lie some common purposes. To ponder them, let's focus on that phrase "mind and spirit." The modest certainties of both must be kept in view. Without an ability to test the spirit by the mind and the mind by the spirit, we run the risk of worshiping a part for the whole. That is the definition of idolatry. In the words of the Unitarian Universalist minister Sara Moores Campbell, "Bringing ourselves into balance requires that we release the faculties of feeling, intuition, and imagination from the pejorative rank as 'emotionalism,' 'mysticism,' and 'fantasy' and integrate them with rational inquiry in the search for the real and the true." In balancing and integrating mind and spirit, Unitarian Universalism has one goal above all others: to make the religious more rational and the rational more religious.

This sense of common purpose is exemplified in people whose personal convictions may at first seem quite diverse. A staunch religious humanist like Khoren Arisian, minister emeritus of the First Unitarian Society in Minneapolis, Minnesota, and former leader of the Ethical Culture Society in New York City, finds most "God-talk" something he can live without. His religious response to life is rooted in nature and the human mind. But Arisian does not hesitate to speak about spirit and spirituality. "Spirituality," he writes, "is a potential aspect of all life. It's not a given quantum, nor is it to be found in exclusive places. We bring it into existence through the relational dimensions of our being. The spirit when it's unlocked moves us towards others [and] helps us feel responsible for the well-being of the world."

On the other hand, a reverent Unitarian Universalist

Christian is as likely to stress the importance of mind in religion as Arisian is to invoke the spirit. The late Wallace W. Robbins, a leader in our Unitarian Universalist Christian Fellowship, grounded his convictions and his spirituality in biblical theology. But he did not hesitate to speak of reason, as did William Ellery Channing, as a gift of God to be applied in understanding and appropriating the truest spirit of that heritage. As Robbins wrote in a reading widely used in our churches:

Ours is a church of reason—not because the mind is free of errors, but because the dialogue of mind with mind, and mind with itself, refines religious thought.

Ours is a church of moral work—not because we think morality is a sufficient religion, but because we know no better way of showing our gratitude to God, and our confidence in one another.

Ours is a church of conscience—not because we hold that conscience is infallible, but because it is the meeting place of God and the human spirit.

Ours is a non-creedal church—not because we have no beliefs, but because we will not be restrained in our beliefs.

We may differ widely in our personal religious orientations, but the sense of common purpose in relating mind and spirit is all-inclusive. Unitarian Universalists like the Reverend Barbara Hebner, a member of the UU Buddhist Fellowship, point out that for practitioners of Buddhist meditation, the terms "spirituality" and "mindfulness" become synonymous. When walking, the goal is to be mindful of walking; when sitting, to be mindful of sitting; when speaking to another person, to be mindful of speaking to that person. An empirical and searching approach to truth follows the example of the Buddha, who tried many paths on the way to enlightenment.

I often describe myself as a *biblical* humanist. I find the religion *about* Jesus distracting and divisive, but I am persistently drawn toward the spirit, example, and religion *of* Jesus. The spiritual disciplines I cultivate include service, study, prayer, meditation, and sharing in congregational worship. Like most Unitarian Universalists, I respect those whose spirituality may differ from my own, convinced that what we have in common is likely to be far more important than anything that may divide us.

A great scholar of world religions, the late Mircea Eliade, based his lifelong study of the wide variety of human religious responses on a similar conviction. In an interview just before he died, he spoke about the need for a "new humanism," grounded not just in reason (where each human mind says, "I am, and I believe—or disbelieve"), but in the recognition of a universal spirituality, infinitely various in its creativity.

"Spirit is strange," Eliade said. "It has an obligation to create."

Of course, human beings can also be "strange." Faced with the mysteries of life and death, in the name of the spirit we can create religious responses that are more fearful and self-serving than they are faithful and inclusive. This is why we do well to keep our rational and critical faculties in play. Religious humanism recognizes a critical humility. So does the biblical tradition. "Little children, keep yourselves from idols" (1 John 5:21). "The Spirit is the source of our life; let it also direct our course" (Gal. 5:25). "But do not trust any and every spirit, my friends, test the spirits, to see whether they are from God" (1 John 4:1). "[For] the harvest of the Spirit is love, joy, peace, patience, kindness, fidelity, gentleness and self-control" (Gal. 5:22).

The ultimate measure of our lives and traditions, beliefs and communities, has yet to be taken. "By their fruits shall ye know them," the Gospel tells us (Matt. 7:20). But this much seems certain: it will depend on a sound integration of our minds and spirits. For this, honoring the results of scientific inquiry is vital. As Ralph Waldo Emerson once said, "The religion that is afraid of science dishonors God and commits suicide. It acknowledges that it is not equal to the whole of truth, that it legislates and tyrannizes over a village of God's empire, but it is not the universal immutable law. Every influx of atheism, of skepticism, is thus made useful as a mercury pill assaulting and removing a diseased religion, and making way for truth."

Unitarian Universalists have a distinguished heritage of honoring science. There is less difference than might be supposed between honest research and devout adoration. We have nurtured many who have known that truth: Joseph Priestley, the eighteenth century scientist-minister who discovered oxygen; Maria Mitchell, who in the nineteenth century was the first important woman astronomer; and in the twentieth century, Charles Steinmetz, the immigrant electrical engineer, and Lewis Howard Latimer, the African-American inventor who worked with Thomas Edison on incandescent lighting. From well before the time of Darwin (who was raised in a British Unitarian family), Unitarian Universalists have had nothing to fear from scientific discovery. Today, we sponsor important annual conferences on science and religion. Dr. Ralph Burhoe, the Unitarian Universalist scholar who founded *Zygon*, a leading journal in the field of religion and science, was even honored by the Templeton Foundation with what is called "the Nobel Prize for progress in religion."

As important as science is, however, a sound integration of mind and spirit means that the world cannot be saved by mind alone, nor by science alone, nor by reason, nor by technology. As our nuclear age and our ecological crisis so painfully demonstrate, without a larger sense of purpose and relatedness, the products of science and the human mind can themselves become dangerous idols. These relational issues, and issues of purpose, are *spiritual* in character. One reason that so many people today say, "I believe in spirituality, but not in religion," is that the products of the human spirit, the various religious traditions, can so easily become warring sects if not brought within a wider, more reasoned perspective. Unitarian Universalism offers the opportunity not only to deepen one's personal spirituality through dialogue, but to do so in a context where "the guidance of reason and the results of science" are honored.

Sadly, most public understanding of the relationship of science to religion is still at a rather primitive level. Frederick Buechner compares most arguments between exponents of faith and science over the nature of the universe to "a conversation between a poet and a podiatrist. The poet says that Suzy walks with beauty like the night. The podiatrist says that Suzy has fallen arches." It won't do only to treat Suzy (or the universe) as defective. The cure may be worse than the disease. Nor will it do simply to express our love for her through poetry and religion. We need a holistic treatment that can recognize the limitations and strengths of both approaches—of science, with its objective, analytic methods; and of religion, with its subjective, evocative visions of the human spirit's place within the whole. Together, the two remind us that ultimate objectivity is not humanly available, even through science. It too uses metaphor. Yet all the high guesses of religion and metaphysics may not, after all, be merely subjective.

In the twentieth century, one attempt to forge an integrated metaphysic is to view reality as *process*. Modern physics teaches that the basic units of reality are not material objects or even energy. Alfred North Whitehead called them "actual events," interdependent through time and tied to the minds, the subjects, that perceive them. He took the position that if there is an "objective" reality, there must be something like an "objective" mind—the thought of God. But too often our thinking, about both religion and science, is still tied to an outdated materialism or an all-too-human idealism.

In a downtown Boston Unitarian church, Whitehead, the mathematician turned religious philosopher, gave his famous lectures on "Religion in the Making." He said that "there is a creative tendency in the universe to produce worthwhile things, and moments come when we can work with it and it can work through us. But the tendency in the universe to produce worthwhile things is by no means omnipotent. Other forces work against it. This creative principle is everywhere. It is a continuing process. Insofar as you partake of this creative process you partake of the divine and that participation is your immortality, reducing the question of whether your individuality survives the death of the body to the estate of irrelevancy. Our true destiny as co-creators in the universe is our dignity and our grandeur."

This philosophy suggests one facet of contemporary Unitarian Universalist theology. In fact, the leading interpreter of process thinking today is Dr. Charles Hartshorne, a Unitarian Universalist in Austin, Texas, and author of *Omnipotence and Other Theological Mistakes*. His many books explore an understanding of God as the supreme example of "social reality," and he is numbered among the most widely respected of contemporary metaphysicians.

Nonetheless, to join a Unitarian Universalist congregation does not require our acceptance of his or any other metaphysical view of reality. On the contrary, we Unitarian Universalists have always united more on the basis of what Channing called "practical religion" than we have on any particular metaphysic or doctrine. By practical we mean supporting one another in our ethical and spiritual living, attempting to bear witness to our highest values in our everyday lives, and in that way having a positive influence on community life. Our religion does not mean demanding a theoretical, spiritual, or mental conformity.

Where other religious movements have long traditions of explicit, even dogmatic teaching—about the nature of God, Jesus, immortality, and revelation—Unitarian Universalism insists upon remarkably little. We are left free to believe not what we *want* to believe but what we find we *must* believe. The Reverend Kathy Fuson Hurt says that this "center of silence" in our tradition reminds her of a phrase in the Hindu scriptures, "that from which words turn back, not having attained." Though we may at times feel hampered by our movement's lack of neat, readily available, and authorized statements on ultimate matters, most of us eventually find in the openness of our faith a quiet humility that encourages our own clarification of the inner life. This practice contrasts dramatically with both the creeds of orthodoxy and the certainties professed by some other heterodox faiths.

Other forms of postconventional religion are more explicitly and doctrinally metaphysical. Emphasizing spirit, metaphysical faith has often taught that the world *is* spirit. Still other reactions to orthodoxy have put the accent on mind, emphasizing ethical rationalism and remaining skeptical toward all theology and metaphysics. Since the Enlightenment, both alternatives have developed on parallel tracks, neither far, historically, from the edges of both Unitarianism and Universalism.

In the rationalist tradition, there are Thomas Paine, the eighteenth-century revolutionary author of *Common Sense* and *The Age of Reason*, and the free-thinkers and debunkers of religious pietism, such as the great nineteenth-century orator Robert Ingersoll. In the twentieth century, the philosopher Bertrand Russell and the modern militant atheist Madelyn Murray O'Hair are part of this group. Institutional manifestations of this rationalist stream include Felix Adler's Ethical Culture movement and the American Humanist Association. These voices speak for "mind."

Speaking for "spirit" is the metaphysical tradition. From the eighteenth century, it includes Emmanuel Swedenborg, whose writings inspired both William Blake and Ralph Waldo Emerson. In the nineteenth century, its proponents included spiritualists with their seances and theosophists with their attempts to integrate Eastern wisdom and Western gnosticism. From the same period the tradition includes Mary Baker Eddy, who was influenced by Unitarian and Universalist thinkers, but pushed beyond the transcendentalists to more dogmatic claims for healing. She taught that sin, death, evil, and illness are not ultimately real, but only illusions of "mortal mind." Today, the institutional manifestations of metaphysical faith include not only Christian Science, but also its offshoots, Religious Science and Unity (formerly the

Unity School of Christianity). (Sometimes we Unitarian Universalists are confused with Unity, or with the Unification Church. But we are quite different.)

I once sat at a luncheon with a Unity minister and a rabbi. "Tell me," said the rabbi, "how do you deal with the problem of evil?"

"Oh," replied the Unity leader, "it's all *maya*"—a Buddhist term, meaning "illusion."

"Try telling that to my Holocaust survivors," said the rabbi.

When I say that in its spirituality Unitarian Universalism is more practical than metaphysical, one of the things I mean is that we have never denied the reality of such things as sin, death, evil, and suffering. Our humanitarian work testifies to this. So does the honesty about death that marks our memorial services. When someone dies we are honest about the physical reality of loss and respond with grief, yet we continue to affirm the spirit of love, which does not die.

Today's New Age spirituality often emphasizes metaphysical teaching. It promotes holism, attunement to the universe, awareness of the divine within, and a variety of methods for spiritual self-realization. In reasserting the interdependence of all existence, the New Age movement has much to commend it. But in a society where individual consumerism increasingly expands to religion and its substitutes, one should be a prudent and wary shopper among the varied New Age books, workshops, ideas, and programs. The product, for one thing, is not always all that "new." Invented ancient wisdom; magical reliance on teachers, pyramids, crystals, or Ouija boards; opportunities for various forms of self-delusion (about one's "past lives," for example) all come mixed with forms of outright spiritual exploitation and manipulation. One may also grow weary of the lack of any practical or down-to-earth social dimension to uplifting "spiritual" lectures, aimed largely at individual attitudes, success, or healing. Without denying the popularity of the message, or the spiritual hunger it represents, we need to be aware, as Unitarian Universalist ethicist and theologian James Luther Adams once put it, that "nothing is ever quite so saleable as egoism wrapped in idealism."

Unitarian Universalism may represent the use of the critical mind in religious matters, but it is not merely that. It is also a community of spirituality—practical and down-to-earth in its personal and civic implications. No matter how much we value the use of reason, no matter how lofty our spiritual ideals, our common concern is to bring those ideals down to earth and into practice in our daily human lives. Morally, we recognize that our lives are mortared together by our common mortality. The words *human* and *humane* both come from the same Latin root, *humus*, the earth that bears us, to which we all return and on which we are asked to walk together in humility during the time that is ours. We may be open-minded, but we recognize with G. K. Chesterton that "the object of opening the mind, as of opening the mouth, is to shut it down again on something solid." Our dialogue with one another is aimed at shaping a solid and practical way of life—one that balances mind and spirit, and devotes both to promoting justice, inspiring deeds of mercy, and reminding one another to walk together humbly before and within a Mystery that transcends us all.

PART 6

Spiritual teachings of Earth-centered traditions which celebrate the sacred circle of life and instruct us to live in harmony with the rhythms of nature.

For the Beauty of the Earth

Forrest Church

From all that dwells below the skies,
Let faith and hope with joy arise,
Let beauty, truth, and good be sung
Through every land by every tongue.
            —*Unitarian Universalist doxology*

PERHAPS THE BEST THING about being a Unitarian Universalist is that when we learn new things we are encouraged to update our point of view. By definition, ours is a non-doctrinal faith. In fact, the term "doctrinaire liberal" is an oxymoron—one cannot be dogmatic and liberal at the same time. If orthodoxy (which literally means "right teaching") proclaims a single, authorized set of answers, we celebrate instead the open mind. We trust that our own thoughts and experiences can be as illuminating as the thoughts and experiences of those who came before us. Not that our answers will therefore be superior. We simply hold that no single book, no revelation, ancient or modern, contains the whole truth. Since for us revelation is not sealed, Unitarian Universalists are free to range broadly in search for answers to age-old questions. Religious liberalism does not require fidelity to the latest fashion, only to remaining open to new sources of inspiration. The newly designed, sixth source of our faith—Earth-centered religious traditions—is a perfect case in point.

Though it elicited considerable debate before being added to our "Purposes and Principles" by the General Assembly in 1995, the sixth source holds a long-established place in our theological tradition. The most revered nineteenth-century Unitarians—Ralph Waldo Emerson, Margaret Fuller, and Henry David Thoreau—wouldn't have blinked at this addition to our covenant. Transcendentalists were liberal both in their openness to new ways of thinking and in their respect for those who had broken past codes, melding old insights into their venture to formulate new ones. In addition, nature shaped their theological vision, drawing them out of narrow academic chambers to view a broader text for contemplation. Of all we subscribe to in our covenant, the seventh principle ("respect for the interdependent web of being of which we are all a part") and its corollary, our new sixth source, may best describe what Emerson, Fuller, and Thoreau held most sacred. Even as the Psalmist celebrates "the earth and the fullness thereof," for their own experience of the Holy our Transcendentalist forebears looked first to the creation.

This said, my own appreciation for Earth-centered theology is both of recent vintage and undoubtedly incomplete. Several years ago, my staff was mocking up the ad sheet for our weekly advertisement in the *New York Times*. I had been joking in the office about a possible opening stanza for the quintessential politically correct hymn. How about this: "I love you, you love me, let's go out and hug a tree." Unable to resist the temptation, my secretary entitled the sermon in our mock ad, "Trees I Have Known and Hugged." The *Times* took this as gospel and ran it. For those of you who want to save money because no one reads church ads, forget it. I even got a call from John Buehrens in Boston. As designated preacher every "Earth Day" when he served with me at All Souls, he wanted to know if I had gone soft.

I have. Ever since Mayor Giuliani appointed me Chair of the Council on the Environment of New York City in 1995, I have devoted a fair portion of my time to protecting and enhancing little environmental treasures in the midst of a vast human ecosystem. Admittedly, as my mother pointed out to me, "the environment of New York City" may strike outsiders as a bit of an oxymoron. My mother can be forgiven. She is from Idaho. If Idaho were as densely packed as Manhattan, all the people in the world could live there. You could empty China into the desert and India into the potato fields, put America in the greater Boise metropolitan area and, after leveling the peaks and building a few million high-rises, accommodate everyone else in what used to be the mountains. Yet, in contrast to Idaho's mountain majesty, though the natural environment of New York City is circumscribed by asphalt and over-shadowed by mighty towers, for this very reason, since value lies in scarcity, what little of nature remains in the midst of our city-scape is, acre for acre, exponentially more valuable. In my environmental work, I am following in the tradition of two nineteenth-century All Souls members, William Cullen Bryant and Peter Cooper. The famous poet and prominent architect led the fight to make Frederick Law Olmsted's dream of Central Park a reality.

Even so, to gain a full appreciation for the sacred in nature, we must leave the city, turn off the artificial lights, and search for stars. Recently, my family and I took a white-water rafting trip down the Middle Fork of the Salmon River. The Middle Fork runs for a hundred miles and is entirely contained within the Frank Church River of No Return Wilderness Area, a 2.2-million-acre stretch, the largest wilderness area in the continental United States. Having long considered being born in Idaho an accident (I am uncomfortable around guns and horses), I was surprised by the power of this homecoming. I looked through my father's eyes and discovered the beauty of things he worked to save, our wild and scenic rivers, our precious wilderness. What saved *me* is that the mountains, rapids, and heavens made me smaller, so small that I began to notice things far bigger than my own little concerns. I was a part of, not apart from, the ground of our being. Its power was real, my own derivative and unimportant. In the ultimate sense, books didn't matter. Churches didn't matter. I heard the cosmos sing and watched nature dance. This was religion.

On my father's tombstone in Boise we placed the following words from one of his speeches: "I never knew a person who felt self-important in the morning after spending the night in the open on an Idaho mountainside under a star-studded summer sky." A lapsed Catholic and secular humanist, my father may have been unchurched, but he was not unacquainted with the one thing churches hope to offer—a chance to walk on holy ground. In his case, Native Americans had walked the ground dedicated in his name long before him. Their paintings decorate, even illuminate, the walls of caves. Their gods were present there, then and now. Anyone looking for the holy land might best begin with the earth that sustains us.

Our denomination's sixth source may have been an official latecomer, but it holds a primary place in our faith's typology. A sense of the earth as a touchstone of the sacred, indeed as holy ground, comes before Judaism and Christianity, before the other world religions, before all the philosophers of humanism. One sure proof of authentic religious experience is the combination of humility and awe. Our encounter with nature inspires both. Though Earth-centered traditions range from simple to complex, from tribal to universal, each taps a power that no book or creed can begin to approximate—the power of the creation. This is true even of the simplest faith—man, woman, fire, food, sun, rain, star. Early animists felt the earth and all its powers—thunder, lightening, floods, volcanoes—to be alive, even divine. Their awe ran the gamut from awesome to awful—from wondrous to terrifying.

We may fairly describe our ancient ancestors' worship and fear of nature's gods as primitive religion. One would think that an enlightenment tradition would celebrate having graduated from so-called superstition and never look back. For many years we did. Yet, in recent years many Unitarian Universalists have begun to discover that with each gain in scientific understanding, we must risk losing something even more important: an intimate experience of the power and mystery of the creation.

Most Unitarian Universalists are immune to the theological temptation toward irrationalism. Irrational beliefs are those that can be disproved by facts. But, tapping our Transcendentalist roots, we are beginning, once again, to acknowledge that much of our experience, and everything that lies beyond our experience, defies rational analysis. Most sacred clues, hints from dream journeys, lovemaking and stargazing, spring from deep within the transrational realm. Though we can in such ways experience a tiny portion of ultimate reality, this reality is neither fathomable nor imaginable. We cannot pin it down or mount it as a trophy on the wall of human knowledge. All we can do is return from our journeys with symbols, metaphors, and stories—the basic building blocks of religion.

If we exclude the transrational realm from our field of contemplation, we delude ourselves. We may begin to presume that we understand, even control, powers completely beyond our control and understanding. We then lose our sense of humility, taking the creation for granted, rather than receiving it, with fear and trembling, as an undeserved, unfathomable gift. Whenever knowledge supplants mystery, our imagination and sense of wonder are just as likely to die as are the gods we pride ourselves for disbelieving. Having dismissed the supernatural, we may miss discovering the *super* in the natural.

This need not be. One need not accept the tenets of ancient animism to perceive heaven in a mustard seed or a world in a grain of sand. To do so is not to reject rationalism, or even skepticism, which guards us from irrational delusion. Thoughtful people can maintain an eye both critical and open. Turning for inspiration to Earth-centered spirituality is not to abandon our critical faculties, but to open them wider, to place ourselves in a larger field and that field under the widest canopy of stars we can imagine. Then, like the first humans, for a sacred moment we too may be terrified and filled with awe. We too may experience raw religion.

William F. Shultz, past president of the Unitarian Universalist Association, speaks less often of God than of "the Holy." This is not merely inclusive rhetoric. Answering a question asked hundreds of years ago by Saint Lawrence—"Whom should I adore: the Creator or the Creation?"—Shultz writes: "Most Western religions have answered back, 'Adore the Creator!' and supplied an image (Zeus, Jehovah, Christ) to be adored. But our answer is far different. Whom should we adore? The Creation, surely, for whatever there be of the Creator will be made manifest in Her handiwork."

Developing this insight, one distinction between Unitarian Universalism and the major scripture-driven Western religions is that we tend to view the world as a school rather than as a corrections facility. Rather than punishing us as sinners by incarcerating us here, sentencing us to life, and then, at death, offering release only to those who have followed a strict set of guidelines for rehabilitation, our faith celebrates the creation not only as a beloved home, but also as a sacred text from which we may draw wisdom. Earth-centered traditions are therefore a natural source for Unitarian Universalism. We may claim no inside knowledge of the creator, but we are quick to affirm, learn from, and protect the creation. "The gods and goddesses—or, if you prefer, the most precious and profound—are accessible to us in the taste of honey and the touch of stone," Bill Shultz writes. "This is why we love the earth, honor the human body, and bless the stars. Religion is not just a matter of things Unseen. For us the Holy is not hidden but shows its face in the blush of the world's exuberance."

One thing that confuses people about Unitarian Universalism—both people of faith and people who reject organized religion—is that we encourage our adherents to experience the Holy wherever they find it, to follow their own soul maps rather than some road map drawn by a higher authority. This explains both the wide-ranging sources for our faith and also our ability to journey together without marching in one prescribed direction. Knowing that we need not think alike to love alike, we acknowledge the integrity of spiritual insights that differ from our own, so long as our neighbor returns the favor. Accordingly, in many Unitarian Universalist congregations the theological compass will range from theist to humanist, from Christian to Jew to Buddhist to pagan, from cosmic pantheist to agnostic, even atheist. Over the years I have come to realize that our covenant with one another is guided more by common values than by common beliefs.

One person who helped me understand how contrasting symbols can point to a remarkably similar reality is Margot Adler. A distinguished author and National Public Radio correspondent, Margot is a priestess of Wicca, a member of the board of advisers of the Covenant of Unitarian Universalist Pagans, and a member of my congregation. The All Souls liturgy is only slightly changed from the liberal Protestant services of a century ago. When I asked Margot why she chose All Souls, she told me that she loves the ritual. It creates a sacred space for her within which she can worship. Through our discussions, despite differences in the letter of our theologies, I have discovered so close a spirit that I understand how she is able to translate from one sacred liturgy to another and find meaning in the universals that connect them. It is important to remember this as we continue to develop from a faith that first took wings in the Protestant reformation to one that encompasses an increasingly diverse complement of inspirational sources. Even as one can say much the same thing in various languages, Unitarian Universalists express like religious values in a wide range of apparently conflicting symbol systems.

Margot's faith is grounded in nature and nature's

goddesses. It is an ancient faith, reaching back to the first agricultural communities, when hunters and gatherers settled in farm-centered villages and began to raise their own food. With cultivation, the earth as a source of life embodied a new set of powers. Once sowing and reaping were at the heart of our survival and our source of fecundity, the divine took on a more personal face, the Goddess, symbol of fertility, giver of life and death. Margot found her way to this source of spiritual insight through her reading of nature writers, people like Henry David Thoreau, Loren Eiseley, and Rachel Carson. "As I read these writers, I was having what I can only describe now as religious feelings," Margot recalls. "I saw that this literature was about our whole relationship to the universe; it showed that everything was interconnected."

This sense of connectedness distinguishes Unitarian Universalism from many other faiths, where one true path leads in a separate direction from other false ones. It accommodates a variety of cosmic claims, while holding us to cosmic connections. "I chose Unitarian Universalism because I need to live in balance," Margot wrote in a recent statement of faith. "I can do all those wonderful, earth-centered spiritual things: sing under the stars, drum for hours, create moving ceremonies for the changes of seasons or the passage of time in the lives of men and women. But I also need to be a worldly, down-to-earth person in a complicated world—someone who believes oppression is real, that tragedies happen, that chaos happens, that not everything is for a purpose. Unitarian Universalism gives me a place to be at home with some of my closest friends: my doubts." At home with our doubts, we can live more companionably with one another. Mysteriously born, fated to die, we are bound to one another by the mortar of mortality. Despite our many differences, we are one.

This intimacy has profound theological significance. We are one with all that lives. As the Unitarian Universalist minister Marni Harmony writes, "I say that it touches us . . . that the seed of our bodies is scarcely different from the same cells in a seaweed, and that the stuff of our bones is like the coral."

Such a worldview has ethical consequences as well. It is no surprise that Earth-centered traditions place a high value on protecting the environment, on saving the Earth. This commitment is manifest in Biblical texts also, especially the prophets, whose words have inspired generations of Unitarian Universalists to work for peace, justice, and environmental protection. As the prophet Isaiah warned twenty-five centuries ago, "The earth dries up and withers, the world languishes and withers, the heavens languish together with the earth. The earth lies polluted under its inhabitants; for they have transgressed laws, violated the statutes, broken the everlasting covenant." If the letter here differs from that of the Earth-centered traditions, the spirit is the same. Again, common values transcend constrasting beliefs. Different sources flow into the same river, which flows into the one cosmic sea. This is the very essence of Universalism, where all that live are related to the one source, itself the wellspring of salvation.

The Unitarian Universalist minister David Bumbaugh expresses this commitment eloquently with reference both to environmental activism and to our Unitarian Universalist belief in the interdependent web of existence, of which we are a part. "We are called to define the religious and spiritual dimensions of the ecological crisis confronting the world," he writes, "and to preach the gospel of a world where each is part of all, where every one is sacred, and every place is holy ground, where all are children of the same great love, all embarked on the same journey, all destined for the same end." Unlike those religions that view the world as a charnel house from which we must escape, Unitarian Universalism reveres the creation and challenges us to nurture it, even to defend it against ourselves when we lose our sense of intimacy with the earth as the ground of our being, the living web that connects us.

Among the little band of vacationers who traveled with my family down the Middle Fork of the Salmon River was an astronomer. On our last night together he gave us a guided tour of the heavens. After pointing out the landmarks, Arcturus, Mars, the Big Dipper, he reminded us that all we can see with the naked eye—it seemed like a thousand stars—is only an infinitesimal part of the universe. Not only are there more than a hundred billion stars in our galaxy, there are an estimated hundred billion galaxies. To bring this down to size, if the universe were a vast beach, our sun would be no larger than a grain of sand and the Earth a tiny speck of dust upon it. So there we were, thirty humans on a beach gazing out into infinitude, experiencing both humility and cosmic awe.

This experience confirmed my faith as a Unitarian Universalist. No difference that divides us comes close to all that unites us on this tiny speck of living dust on a single grain of sand on the vast beach of the creation. We are truly kith and kin, brothers and sisters, children of a great and magnificent mystery. Holding hands together with my family and fellow travelers as the earth circled our little star coursing through the heavens, I felt two things more profoundly perhaps than ever before: We are one, and we are blessed.

Returning to the Springs

John A. Buehrens

The dramatic action that we need to create a way of life on Earth that really works will be taken not through personal, social, or political action, but through spiritual action.
  —*Brooke Medicine Eagle, in Buffalo Woman Comes Singing*

The way back is always shorter.
    —*Maya Deren, "The Artist as God in Haiti"*

Ho, everyone who thirsteth; come ye to the waters.
      —*Isaiah 55:1*

LIKE SO MANY in our culture, I went through a period when I did not go to church. When I began to explore spirituality again, I was skeptical about why people need church. Soon I asked the only regular churchgoer I really respected, my grandmother, why she kept going back, Sunday after Sunday.

"Why I go to church?" she replied. "Oh, Janni: *soul*, you know, sometimes get very empty. Faith small, like mustard seed."

I knew enough of her story to know some of what she meant. My grandmother had been orphaned in Eastern Europe before she was ten. She came to America through Ellis Island with only an older sister to meet her in Chicago. There she met and married another orphan. They had four children. But by the end of the influenza epidemic of 1919, she and my grandfather had buried all four babies. Soul get very empty indeed.

That was when my grandfather stopped going to church—when it seemed his wife was going to die as well, the priest wouldn't come to the house to give her the last rites. Then, in the Great Depression, with three more children's mouths to feed, Grampa lost his factory job. The two had to try to scratch a living out of a patch of dry ground in Texas for nearly two years. During World War II, nearly all their remaining relatives in Slovakia were killed. Faith like mustard seed, indeed.

"When I go to church," said Grandma, "I have to be grateful again, just to be alive. I am there with other people. So I don't think just about my own problems. Many have them, just like me. I pray with them and for them. My thoughts go wider, deeper, higher. Sometimes," she said to me, "does not even matter if priest's sermon is not so very good! None of us can see the future, but I pray for you and your cousins, for all young people. Hope comes back. I pray for your grandfather. Love comes back, too. I go home to show him—not just by words—that is no good in life to stay bitter. I get him to help me do something nice for a child or a neighbor. Dat's why I go back to church every week."

My grandmother seemed to know intuitively what my chosen faith of Unitarian Universalism now helps me to proclaim explicitly: Faith is not ultimately about believing some proposition in spite of the evidence; it is more like living with courage, gratitude, and integrity in spite of life's inevitable losses. And hope is not a matter of knowing that everything will turn out all right, either for oneself, or even for all of us on Earth together. It is more like directing your life toward a point on the horizon beyond which none of us can see, but toward which we all have to journey if there is to be a worthwhile future for any one of us. And finally, love is no mere Hallmark greeting card sentiment: it is more like living here and now, serving justice, doing works of mercy, and walking humbly with one another before a Mystery that transcends us all.

Religion seems to come down to us through history as a rather polluted stream. No lab tests are needed to sense that it has acquired poisonous accretions, products more of human fears than of real faith, added in the form of dogmas aimed at controlling others. In many ways my attitude toward religion is like that of the poet Marianne Moore toward poetry: "I, too, dislike it: there are things that are important beyond all this fiddle." Yet in the midst of it all, I've found, as she did, "a place for the genuine." Genuine reverence and humility, genuine tears of compassion, genuine enduring love for others, and genuine joy in the miracle of Being.

My mentor in learning this, more than anyone else, was the Unitarian Universalist minister and poet Jacob Trapp. "The spirit of good poetry and of authentic religion are the same," Jake would say, "imaginative compassion."

Raised in the Dutch Calvinist church of Western Michigan, Jake was excommunicated as a "free thinker" at the age of nineteen. When he became a free-thinking Unitarian minister, he drew more on poets than on theologians. He taught that the pattern of all true human living is meeting, with its deep rhythm of belonging, breaking away, returning, although never to where one started. In that sense, Thomas Wolfe was right: You can't go home again. Still, our spirits yearn to return to what is unpolluted, authentic and original in human religious experience.

Jake called it "returning to the springs." He found it at the source of all spiritual traditions: mystery, awe, and renewal; basic gratitude for the unmerited beauty of Being itself; faith that isn't dogma, real hope, and enduring love. Jake was never my pastor. When I first knew him, he was retired. I'd spent a year as a student minister in the church where he'd served for a quarter century. "We knew each other before we ever met," he used to say.

Jake had retired to Santa Fe, New Mexico. There he felt an affinity for the land and for the spirituality of the Native people. When May Sarton, another Unitarian poet, visited the Pueblos, witnessed the dances, and heard the songs and prayers, she called it "going back to the rivers that rise in the heart."

When I was installed as minister in Dallas, Jake came to speak. He told of a Pueblo where the priest couldn't abide Native traditions, despised the Corn Dance as "pagan," and had the plaza where it was held paved over for parking. The people unceremoniously ran him out of the Pueblo, put their feet back in touch with Mother Earth, then wrote to the bishop telling him not to send anyone until he found a priest who would respect their customs.

When I drove Jake around Dallas, we paused at the floodplain of the Trinity River, which separates the affluent city's downtown skyline from its poorest neighborhoods. When I disparagingly compared the river's polluted shallowness and episodic flooding to the worst aspects of revivalist religion in the Bible Belt,

Jake quietly pointed out the beautiful herons in the marshes and the poor people fishing from the bridges. Upstream, he reminded me, toward his New Mexico mountains, the river came from life-giving springs, easy to forget but capable of cooling and refreshing the soul, even on the hottest, harshest day.

In the last two decades of his life (he died in his nineties), Jake walked and meditated every morning. Often he carved wood, or wrote a poem. "The fresh mountain springs of religion are in the singing of poems," he said, "in such feelings of wonder, of related-ness, of intimacy with all that lives. Awe becomes reverence. Relatedness becomes community and communion." One of Jake's poems is based on a Native American prayer:

> Great Spirit, whose voice is heard in the stillness,
> whose breath gives life to all,
> we come before you as children
> needing the help of your strength and wisdom.
>
> Give us to walk in beauty,
> seeing the uncommon in the common,
> aware of the great stream of wonder
> in which we and all things move.
>
> Give us to see more deeply
> into the great things of our heritage,

and the simple yet sublime truths
hidden in every leaf and every rock.

May our hands treat with respect
the things you have created.
May we walk with our fellow creatures
as sharing with them the one life that flows from you.

Jake respected the rituals and traditions of those whom Canadians call the First Peoples of this continent. He would have been pleased that Unitarian Universalists have now acknowledged that one of the sources of our chosen faith runs back to the Earth-centered spirituality which precedes all the text-based religions. "To despise the pagan," he would quote the Dutch theologian Cornelis Miskotte as saying, "is to despise the human. Paganism is everyone's first religion."

He himself preferred the term "primitive religion," understood as coming from the Latin *primus*, meaning "first, original, elemental." In the art and culture of the over-mechanized twentieth century, he noted how the "primitive" has often provided the deepest sources of renewal for art, music, poetry and religion. "Return to the source," says a Chinese proverb, "and you find the meaning."

Indigenous religious traditions, of course, can also be misused and distorted. Take Shinto, the traditional

Earth-centered spirituality of Japan. In the years leading up to 1945, Shinto was interpreted in a nationalistic way, and put to the use of an ethnocentric militarism.

That year, 1945, my friend the Reverend Yukitaka Yamamoto came home from the war, sickened by the slaughter. He found that his older brother had been killed and that he was now the ninety-nineth Chief Priest of Shinto's Tsubaki Grand Shrine. Purifying himself each night under the shrine's bone-chilling waterfall in a ritual called *misogi*, Yamamoto swore that he would help to purify Shinto of its nationalistic accretions, returning it to a primal reverence for the spirits, the *kami*, in all nature, in all creatures and people. As a religious activist for dialogue and peace, Yama-moto-*sensei* (teacher) has become a good friend to Unitarian Universalists, serving as president of the International Association for Religious Freedom.

The Unitarians of the Khasi Hills in northeast India are members of that I.A.R.F. Their story seems worth telling here. In the nineteenth century, when all of South Asia came under British dominion, the Khasis were missionized. They are not ethnically related to most Hindus but are a tribal people more probably related to the Khmer of Cambodia. They are matrilineal and had a religious tradition that connected them to both Father Sky and Mother Earth. But most were

converted to Christianity by staunch Calvinist missionaries from England and Wales.

Eventually one of the converts, Harom Kissor
Singh, said to the missionaries, in essence, "Thank you
for introducing us to these profound spiritual and
moral teachings of Jesus. Now please explain this:
Why must we believe so many things *about* Jesus?
When he taught, did he not want us all simply to treat
one another as sisters and brothers, as children of one
God? The one he called 'Father,' that our tribal religion called 'Mother'; the one the Muslims call Allah
and for whom the Hindus have so many names?"

The missionaries were incensed. They didn't quite
say, "Die, heretic!" They just said, "We know your
kind back home. You're a Unitarian!" Kissor Singh
replied, "Oh? Thank you for that, too! It is always
good to know one is not alone in the world! Do
you have that address?" He contacted the British
Unitarians and in 1887 in the town of Shillong,
founded a church dedicated (in the words of Eph. 4:6)
to the "One God and Father of all, who is above all,
and through all, and in you all."

Kissor Singh's rejection of Calvinist creedalism gave
him a way to return to the deepest springs of traditional Khasi spirituality, while still taking what good
he had found in the religion *of* Jesus, not *about* Jesus.
Each Khasi Unitarian church has a free, non-sectarian

school for all the children in its area—because the government has not always provided schools, because the only other alternatives are mission schools, and because they know what we have forgotten: "It takes a whole village to raise a child."

During my time as UUA President (1993-2001), occupying the big front office on the third floor of 25 Beacon Street in Boston, next to the State House and overlooking Boston Common, nothing pleased me more than to stop my work to greet visitors, especially a youth group. Often I was aware that they had come to headquarters in Boston as though "returning to the springs" of our democratic and noncreedal faith.

Opening with my mother's remark on seeing my grand office ("Hm! Don't let it go to your head!"), my tour would begin with the "great cloud of witnesses" hanging on my office walls. Some are famous. There's a profile portrait of Susan B. Anthony, for example. The wellsprings of equality for women in America go back a century and a half to her efforts in upstate New York. When the first Women's Rights Convention was held at Seneca Falls in 1848, it adjourned to the Unitarian Church in Rochester, where the Anthonys were members.

Sometimes I'd point out the window to the statue of Unitarian Horace Mann next door. Religiously concerned that poor children had no right to free, public schools, Mann resigned as president of the Massachusetts Senate in order to organize such schools. I'd point out the monument across the street—the one whose story was told in the movie *Glory*, about the first regiment of ex-slaves, led by the gallant young Unitarian colonel, Robert Gould Shaw, in the fight against slavery. I'd show off the desk that Thomas Starr King carried out to California, to save the gold fields for the Union, which came home with his widow. I'd give directions to the house that Unitarian Louisa May Alcott bought on Beacon Hill with money she made for her impoverished family from *Little Women*.

Especially with youth groups and people new to Unitarian Universalism, my point was to make sure they were aware that they had returned to the springs of American concern for spiritual freedom and equality. The challenge, of course, is to renew that spiritual concern in our own time, in our own lives. It's not just to know the history of this liberating faith tradition and be renewed by it. It's also to know what the faith we have freely chosen teaches: that history is meant to be shaped by all of us, even by those who in the past were pushed around by it.

Sometimes, when people who have been searching for an open and noncreedal religious community finally find us, they ask with some heat, "Where have you been? Why have you been keeping this approach to religion such a secret?"

There's another Beacon Hill story I sometimes tell. It's about a Unitarian *grande dame* at a suffrage rally in the 1890s. A younger woman admired the lady's hat and asked, "Why, wherever did you get such wonderful bonnet?" According to legend, the reply came, "My dear, on Boston's Beacon Hill, Unitarian ladies do not get their hats anywhere; they simply have them!"

The point, of course, is that for too long, at least on the Unitarian side of the family, our faith was treated that way. Great pride was taken in doing no proselytizing. Telling people where they might obtain a liberal and liberating faith was considered vulgar. One either had to inherit the tradition or discover it on one's own.

Fortunately, the Universalist side of the family always knew better. Rather than keep the liberal light under a bushel, they encouraged going out into the highways and byways to offer people "not hell, but hope and courage." And in recent years, since the merger of the Unitarian and Universalist movements in 1961, we have increasingly been willing to do the same. Rather than waiting for our own offspring to return to church only when their own little children shall lead them in search of a decent church school, for example, we have been establishing young adult ministries, with groups in many congregations and at over a hundred colleges and universities.

"Returning" is, after all, something that can, and should, occur over and over again at any stage of life.

Returning to one's best self in community. Returning to a deep sense of spiritual connection to others and to a common source and resource for right living. Returning to a faith that is neither imposed from without nor unchanging, but freely chosen and always seeking to be deepened and nourished.

One aspect of religious living is the steady work of being part of a human community. But there is also an aspect of returning, religiously, which means coming back to the deep wellspring of Being, more accepting and gracious than anyone (including ourselves) who might judge the worth of our working and doing. I love the words of the prophet: "In returning and *rest* shall ye be saved; in quietness and confidence shall be your strength," and "Ho, everyone who thirsteth, come ye to the waters . . ." (Isaiah 30:15 and 55:1)

This is a chosen pilgrimage. If you want simple words to describe it, I commend these, by my friend and colleague, the Reverend Stephen Kendrick:

Our congregations freely gather to live out a democratic faith.

Every human being is holy and is called to the tasks and joys of love.

We do not limit the truth of God (even to the word "God") but live in openness and belief in human freedom and dignity.

Our creed is kindness.

We celebrate the gift of life, and join in taking on the
    sufferings of this fragile world.
We are this generation's bearers of an eternal message,
    drawn from ancient springs, that truth must grow,
    enlarge, and glow in creative freedom.
Revelation is not sealed. It is lived anew in every heart.

"You say you want it simpler?" he asks. Try this:
"We join in celebrating one world, one people, one
love, which is Truth."

It's a tall order, this chosen return to the springs of
faith, but our heritage inspires us and compels us to do
no less. We warmly and cordially invite you to join us.

A Brief Chronology of Unitarian Universalist History

In the Early Church

325 Nicene Creed adopted at the Council of Nicea under the emperor Constantine; establishes the dogma of the Trinity and suppresses the lower Christology espoused by Arius and his followers.

544 Another church council condemns as heresy the belief in universal salvation, a teaching traced back to second-century theologian Origen of Alexandria.

In Reformation Europe

1531 Michael Servetus (1510–53) publishes *On the Errors of the Trinity*.

1539 Katherine Vogel of Krakow, Poland, burned at the stake for denying the Trinity; birth of Faustus Socinus, leader of the Polish unitarian (Socinian) movement (d. 1604).

1553 Servetus burned at the stake in Calvin's Geneva.

1566 Francis David preaches against the doctrine of the Trinity in Transylvania.

1568 King John Sigismund of Transylvania, under the influence of David, issues the earliest edict of religious toleration.

1579 Francis David, condemned as a heretic, dies in prison.

1654 John Biddle, founder of English Unitarianism, banished to the Scilly Islands.

1658 The Polish Diet banishes Socinians.

In Eighteenth-Century England and America

1703 Thomas Emelyn imprisoned at Dublin for anti-Trinitarian beliefs; birth of George de Benneville, early universalist advocate.

1723 De Benneville preaches universalism in Europe; birth of Theophilus Lindsey, later leader of London Unitarians.

1741 De Benneville emigrates to Pennsylvania; birth of John Murray, founder of organized American Universalism.

1770 Murray emigrates to America; preaches in Thomas Potter's chapel at Good Luck, N.J.

1779 First Universalist congregation in America gathered at Gloucester, Mass., with Murray as minister.

1785 Liturgy of King's Chapel, Boston, revised to omit references to the Trinity.

1787 King's Chapel congregation ordains James Freeman as its minister, becoming "Anglican in worship, congregational in polity, and unitarian in theology."

1794 Joseph Priestley, British Unitarian minister and scientist, emigrates to Pennsylvania.

1796 First Unitarian Church of Philadelphia organized with Priestley's encouragement.

In Nineteenth-Century America

1802 The oldest Pilgrim church in America (founded at Plymouth in 1620) becomes unitarian.

1803 Universalists at convention in Winchester, N.H., adopt a confession of faith.

1804 President Thomas Jefferson compiles his own version of the Gospels, inspired by Priestley.

1805 Universalist Hosea Ballou publishes *A Treatise on the Atonement,* rejecting the doctrine of the Trinity; Henry Ware, Sr., a unitarian, elected Hollis Professor of Divinity at Harvard.

1819 William Ellery Channing preaches "Unitarian Christianity" in Baltimore, helps gather first Unitarian Church in New York City.

1825 The American Unitarian Association founded.

1833 The General Convention of Universalists in the United States founded.

1838 Ralph Waldo Emerson's "Divinity School Address" at Harvard.

1841 Theodore Parker's "Transient and Permanent in Christianity" preached in South Boston.

1850 Death of Margaret Fuller, author of *Woman in the Nineteenth Century*.

1863 Ordination of Olympia Brown as Universalist minister, first woman to be regularly ordained by any denomination.

1864 Death of Thomas Starr King, Universalist minister and pastor of the First Unitarian Church of San Francisco, who "saved California for the Union."

1865 National Conference of Unitarian Churches, organized by Henry Whitney Bellows, gives Unitarians a more effective denominational structure.

1866 Organization of the Universalist General Convention (renamed in 1942 the Universalist Church in America).

1867 Organization of the Free Religious Association.

1884 Death of Emerson; American Unitarian Association becomes a congregational and representative body, later absorbing the National Conference; publication of *Ten Great Religions*, by James Freeman Clarke.

1890 Universalists establish churches in Japan.

1893 World Parliament of Religions held in Chicago, organized by Unitarian minister Jenkin Lloyd Jones.

1899 A joint commission first discusses merger of Unitarian and Universalist movements.

In Twentieth-Century America

1900 The International Congress of Free Christians and Other Religious Liberals formed (later the International Association for Religious Freedom).

1902 Beacon Press launched, broadening the American Unitarian Association's publishing program.

1908 Unitarian Fellowship for Social Justice organized by John Haynes Holmes (also a founder of the NAACP, the ACLU, and the Fellowship of Reconciliation).

1917 William Howard Taft, fifth Unitarian president, serves as moderator of the American Unitarian Association.

1921 Universalist women acquire Clara Barton homestead (later a camp for diabetic girls).

1931 Second Commission on Unitarian-Universalist merger.

1935 Washington Statement of Faith adopted by Universalists.

1936 American Unitarian Association Commission on Appraisal issues report.

1937 Frederick May Eliot elected president of AUA (d. 1957).

1939 Unitarian Service Committee organized.

1944 Church of the Larger Fellowship organized to serve Unitarians living in areas without Unitarian congregations.

1950s A. Powell Davies, minister of All Souls, Washington, D.C., inspires the founding of ten suburban congregations; fellowship movement organized under Monroe Husbands.

1961 Unitarian Universalist Association formed, with Dana McLean Greeley as first president.

1963 *Hymns for the Celebration of Life* published.

1965 James Reeb killed at Selma, Alabama.

1969 Robert Nelson West elected second UUA president; controversy over black empowerment vs. integration.

1977 Paul Carnes elected third UUA president; dies in office.

1978 Eugene Pickett elected fourth UUA president.

1985 William F. Schulz elected fifth UUA president; new statement of Principles and Purposes adopted.

1993 John A. Buehrens elected sixth UUA president. Denise Davidoff elected fifth moderator. *Singing the Living Tradition* published.

1995 Statement of principles and purposes amended to include the sixth source, the spiritual teachings of Earth-centered traditions.

Suggestions for Further Reading

Ahlstrom, Sydney E., and Jonathan S. Carey, eds. *An American Reformation: A Documentary History of Unitarian Christianity.* Middletown, Conn.: Wesleyan University Press, 1985. Original documents of American Unitarian Christianity up to the 1880s, with an introductory essay.

Hewett, Phillip. *Unitarians in Canada.* Ontario: Fitzhenry and Whiteside, 1978. An account of the influence of Canadian Unitarianism by the minister of the Unitarian Church in Vancouver.

Jefferson, Thomas. *The Jefferson Bible: The Life and Morals of Jesus of Nazareth.* Boston: Beacon Press, 1989. A new edition of Jefferson's redaction of the Gospels, with essays by F. Forrester Church and Jaroslav Pelikan.

Marshall, George. *The Challenge of a Liberal Faith.* 3d ed. Boston: UUA Skinner House Books, 1987. An affirmation of Unitarian Universalist values, with an account of history and beliefs, by the former minister of the Church of the Larger Fellowship.

Mendelsohn, Jack. *Being Liberal in an Illiberal Age: Why I Am a Unitarian Universalist.* Boston: Beacon Press, 1985. Revised edition of an earlier book, *Why I Am a Unitarian Universalist,* by the president of the Unitarian Universalist Ministers Association.

Morrison-Reed, Mark D. *Black Pioneers in a White Denomination.* Boston: Beacon Press, 1984. An account of early African American leaders in Unitarian Universalism, by the co-minister of the First Unitarian Congregation in Toronto, Ontario.

Parke, David, ed. *The Epic of Unitarianism.* Boston: UUA Skinner House Books, 1984. Original documents from the history of liberal religion, from the sixteenth century to the twentieth.

Robinson, David. *The Unitarians and the Universalists.* Westport, Conn.: The Greenwood Press, 1985. A history of the two religious movements in America, with brief biographies of leaders.

Scholefield, Harry B., ed. *The Unitarian Universalist Pocket Guide.* Boston: UUA Skinner House Books, 1988. Five brief chapters on "Our Beliefs," "Our Caring Communities," "Our Roots," "Our Ways of Worship," "Our Concern for Social Justice," and "Our Ways of Education," with extensive bibliography.

Wesley, Alice Blair. *Myths of Time and History: A Unitarian Universalist Theology.* Privately printed, 1986; available from the UUA Bookstore, 25 Beacon Street, Boston, Mass.,

02108-2800. Traces Unitarian Universalist theology to the Pilgrim doctrine of the covenant.

Williams, George Huntston. *American Universalism: A Bicentennial Historical Essay.* Boston: UUA Skinner House Books, 1983. A typological study of the first one hundred years of American Universalism.

Wright, Conrad, ed. *Three Prophets of Religious Liberalism: Channing, Emerson, Parker.* Boston: UUA Skinner House Books, 1985. Three classic statements of nineteenth-century Unitarian Universalism: William Ellery Channing's "Unitarian Christianity," Ralph Waldo Emerson's "Divinity School Address," and Theodore Parker's "The Transient and the Permanent in Christianity." Introduction by Conrad Wright.